New Tiny Houses

space-saving architecture

Sibylle Kramer

New Tiny Houses

space-saving architecture

BRAUN

Contents

Preface

A tiny house is much more than just a small building. It is a concept of living that can make big dreams come true when we ask ourselves how we want to live in the future. This ranges from the rather banal question of "How can I finance my dream of owning a home?" to more complex questions, such as, "If I sacrifice traditional luxuries, will I gain more freedom?" and even societal considerations, for example, "How do we deal with demographic shifts; how do we want to grow old?" But tiny houses can also provide answers for topics like ecology, sustainability, and efficiency. A considerable challenge for future tiny-house residents – and architects and designers. Because developing one of these small-scale structures also comes with the opportunity to present a certain perspective. In this context, use of resources is just as important as balancing luxury, time, and space. This book depicts 44 superb examples of masterfully implemented tiny-house concepts. The varied ideas and design approaches prove that even – or especially – in the smallest space, it's possible to implement carefully thought-out layouts and living-space concepts without sacrificing the quality of the design. A tiny house offers so many opportunities: It can be mobile, flexible, and expandable. It can be prefabricated and transported by truck. It can be constructed and moved into in no time. Some tiny houses exist as standalone houses, as solitary sculptural structures, while others form a community in a small village. The type of tiny house presented in this book is an affirmation of a conscious way of living and good design. And that is what unites the projects depicted here: They are all the result of consistent and outstanding, precisely thought-out design in a small space. Let them inspire you ...

The ÖÖD Golden House

Different locations

Design
ÖÖD House

Completion & Construction Time
2024 - 6 months

Client
Privat

GFA
26.3 m^2

Design Task
Sophisticated cabins with high-quality designs

Photographer
ÖÖD / Jaan Parmask

The ÖÖD Golden House was designed to offer luxury in nature and features gold-shimmering glass along with refined, gold-colored décor that presents unique products and high-quality design elements. The strictly limited series contains just 79 units that correspond to the atomic number of gold. The golden glass façade changes its appearance throughout the day and the seasons, triggering a dynamic aesthetic appeal. The ÖÖD House consists of a steel frame and an industrial-quality-glass façade, thereby setting the standard for longevity.

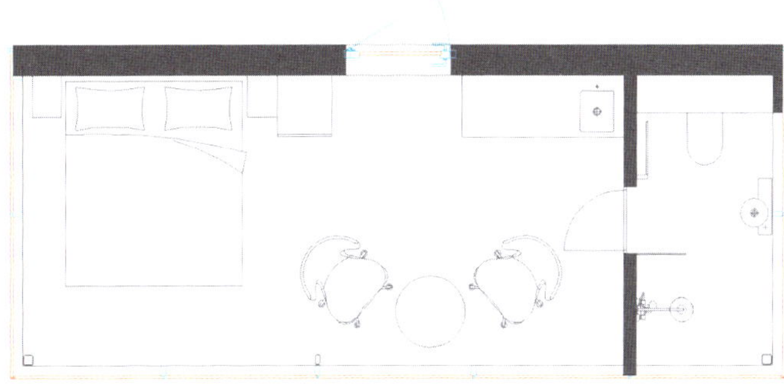

Cabin in Nordmarka

Oslo, Norway

Design
Rever & Drage

Completion & Construction Time
2022 - 24 months

Client
Bjørn Vike and Jo Toftdahl

GFA
29 m^2

Design Task
New functional cabin with old-fashioned charm

Photographer
Tom Auger

This little Cabin in Nordmarka, the wooded wilderness bordering on Oslo, sits right next an older cabin of the same size. Together, they form an angular courtyard that opens up towards the sun and unveils a view to the southwest. The developer was determined to retain the old-fashioned 1930s charm of the main outdoor area – which is why the new cabin's striking new windows resemble the existing ones. A bench in front of the open glass corner offers an undisturbed view of the sunset. The interior presents a simple but functional concept with levels that ascend around the central area.

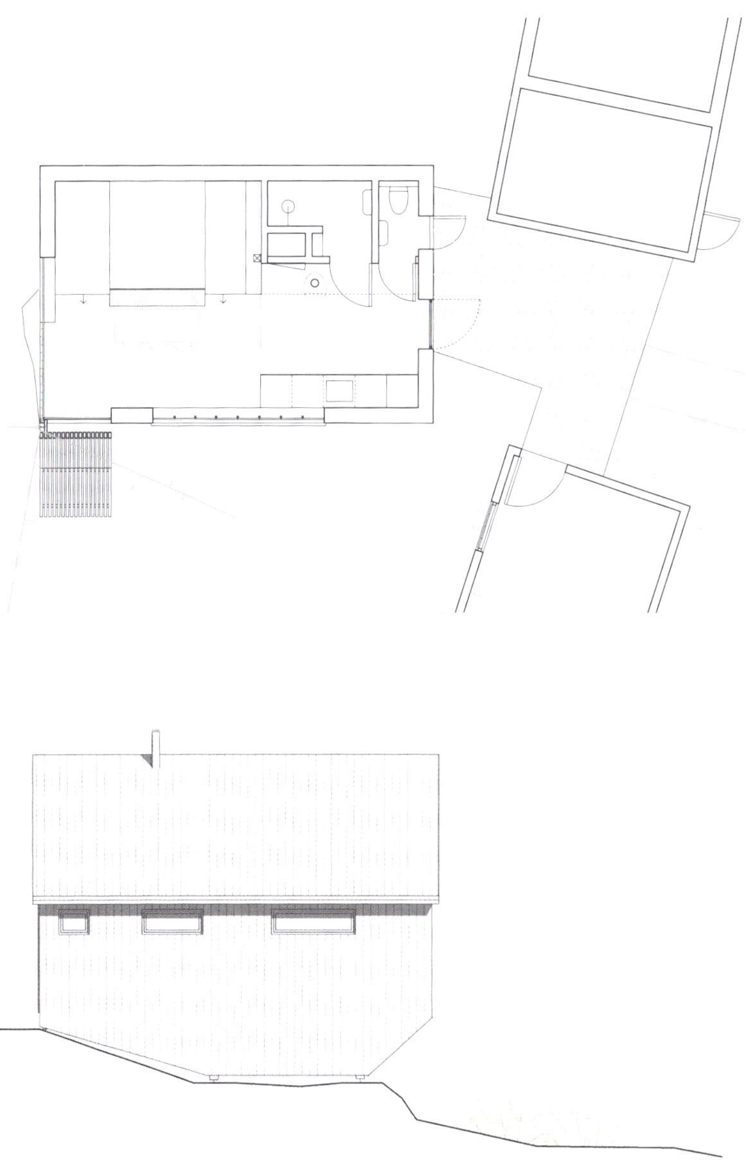

Arcana

Ontario, Canada

Design
Leckie Studio Architecture + Design

Completion & Construction Time
2020 - 16 weeks

Client
Arcana

GFA
16 m^2

Design Task
Self-contained cabins designed to blend invisibly into the surrounding deciduous forest

Photographer
Andrew Latreille Photography

The self-contained cabins are clad with reflective, polished stainless steel and blend into the surrounding deciduous forest to the point of near invisibility. The metal cladding makes use of an innovative, slightly distorted reflective quality to protect birds and wildlife from injury. Every cabin comes with a kitchenette, a queen bed, a bathroom with a shower, a table, an outdoor terrace, and a firepit. The cabins are designed to require as little energy as possible to allow them to be deployed on difficult and remote sites. They can be operated with a small generator as a back-up electricity source. Every structure is designed as a cocoon-like, enclosed environment within the greater natural surroundings.

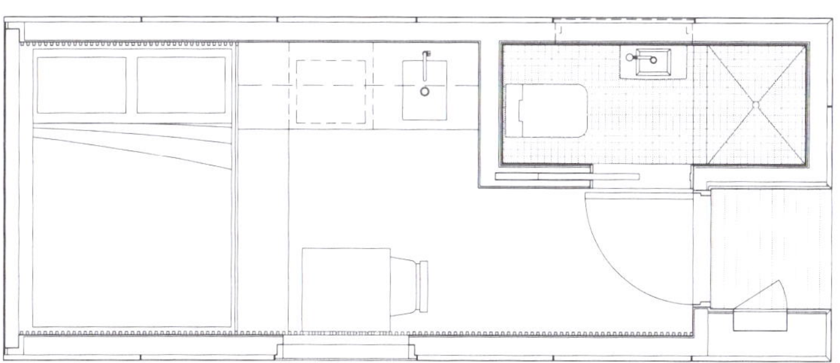

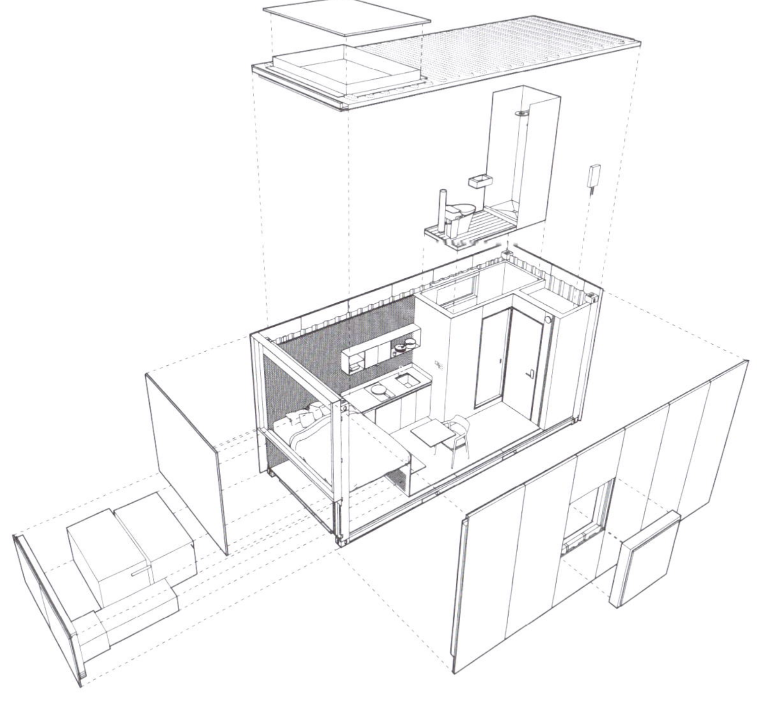

Zen House

Hainburg an der Donau, Austria

Design
Jan Tyrpekl

Completion & Construction Time
2023 - 9 months

Client
Farm Karolinenhof

GFA
32 m^2

Design Task
Archetypal shape on pillars

Photographer
Jakub Hrab

Zen House is located on a farm complex, bordering a young orchard and mature trees. It features an archetypal shape, but stands on pillars together with the terrace, thereby allowing the landscape to flow freely beneath and through the house. Like a bird's nest, the living area sits at a high elevation atop a plateau, exuding a sense of security and intimacy. The interior includes a bar, which is integrated into the furniture and connected to the bed, and a fireplace. Between these elements lies a transition zone with two opposing HS portals that lead to the terrace or to the orchard.

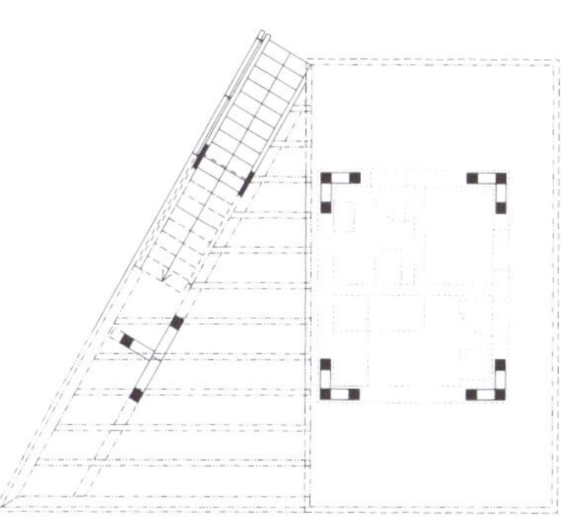

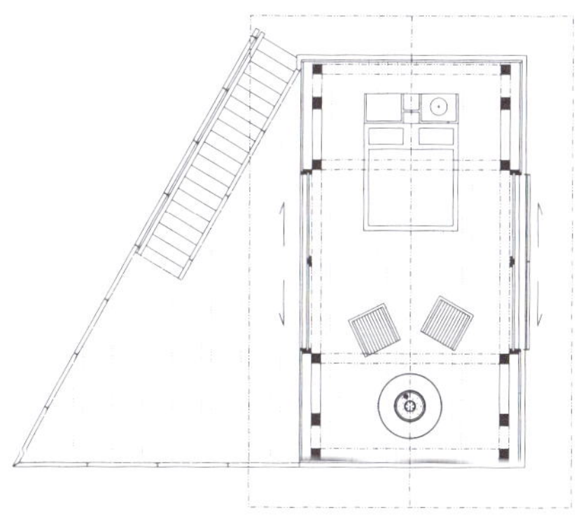

Matamata Cabin

Auckland, New Zealand

Design
Rick Hill

Completion & Construction Time
2022 - 3 months

Client
Rick Hill

GFA
15 m^2

Design Task
Build an off-grid rentable cabin in the middle of nature

Photographer
Ross Keane, Boundless VIsion, Lisa Sun Photography

The cabin is designed as a practical and flexible space, with carefully conceived surfaces and handmade built-in furnishings throughout. Light enters the building from every angle, which, together with the gabled roof, allows the structure to feel much larger than its actual dimensions of 15 square meters. The cabin was built with the goal of making the most out of its rural location and bringing the outdoor space inside. It is completely self-contained, collects rainwater, and powers all devices with solar energy. Key factors of consideration during construction included longevity and sustainability, along with the ultimate sense of comfort and a feeling of subtle luxury.

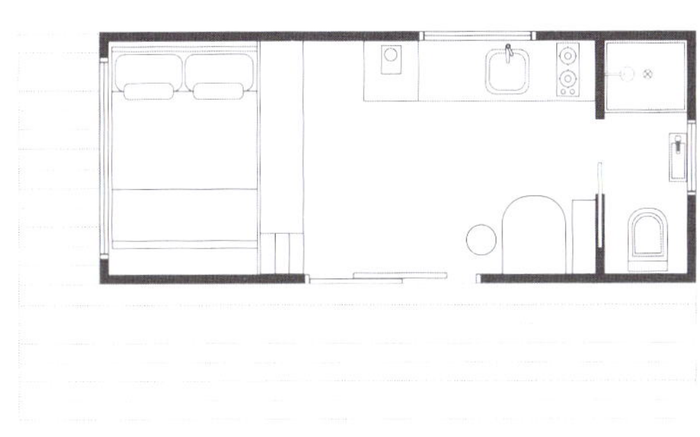

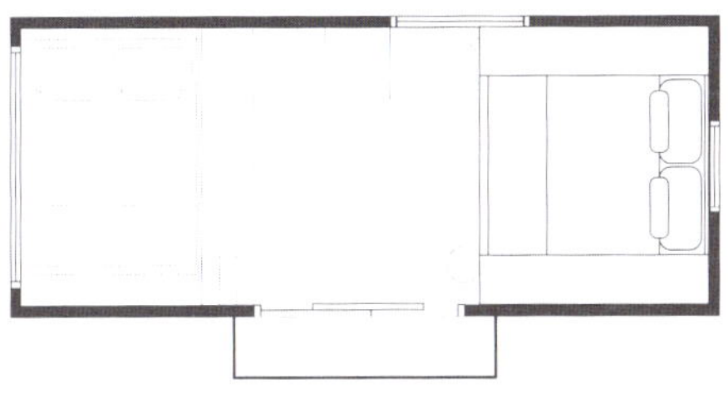

Strandvejen 35

Følle Strand, Denmark

Design
Jesper Kusk Arkitekter

Engineer
Artelia A/S

Completion & Construction Time
2023 - 24 months

Client
Henrik Mortensen

GFA
46 m^2

Design Task
Tiny summer house inspired by fisherman's houses

Photographer
Hampus Berndtson

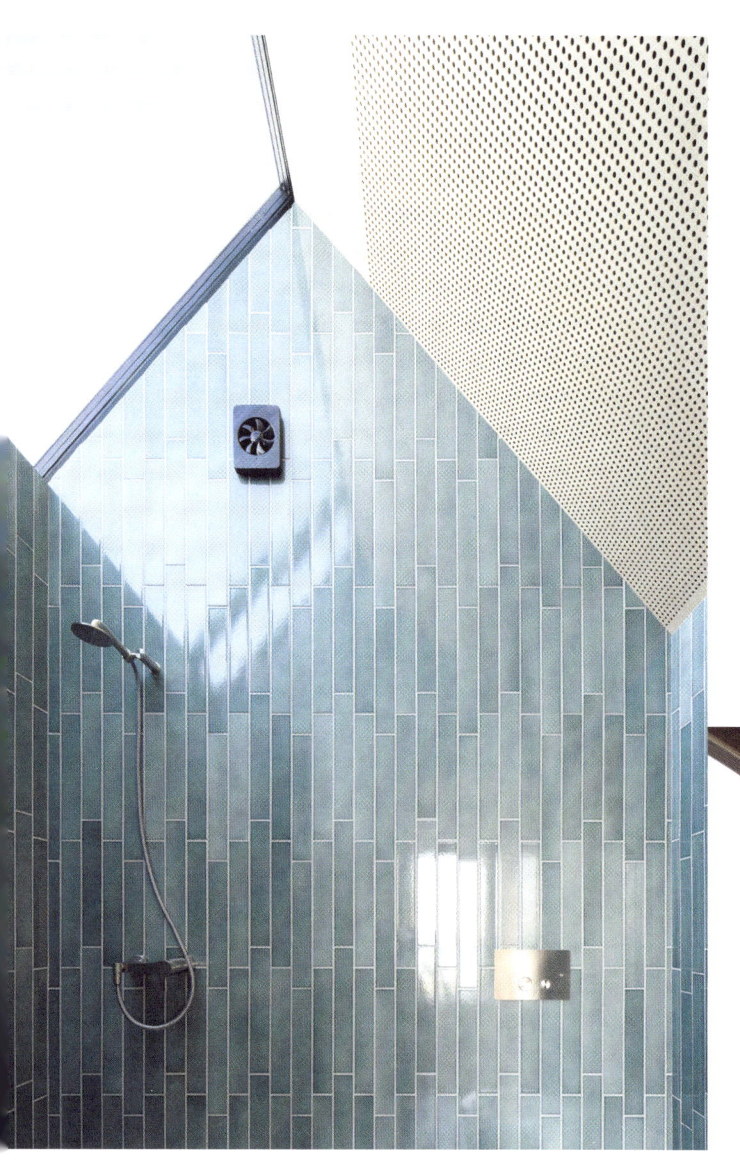

A tiny summer house stands in Følle Strand, inspired by the area's characteristic and historic fisherman's houses. The goal was to create a scaled and well-adapted built environment with three juxtaposed little structures that overlook the bay of Kalø. Measuring just 46 optimized square meters, the house accommodates a total of seven sleeping spaces. Here, windows and passageways turn into living areas, and sliding doors between the staggered structures separate the interior rooms. Wood serves as the primary construction material for the summer house. The façades and the roof are covered with Danish oak, the color and material of which harmonizes with the location.

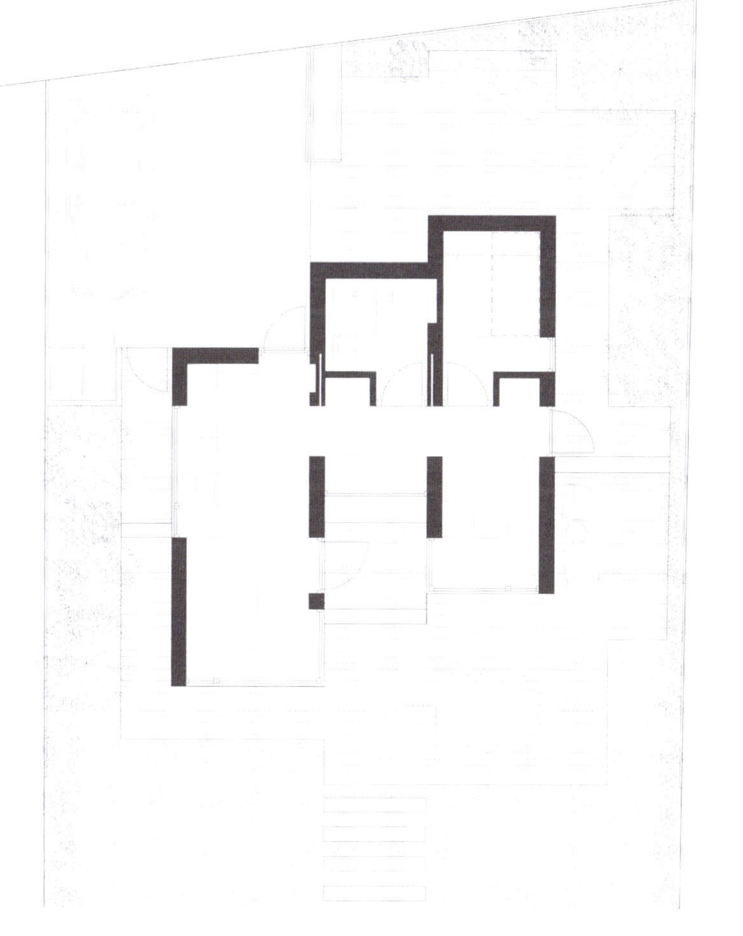

Lost Whiskey Cabin

Virginia, USA

Design
GreenSpur
Mark Turner and Zach Gasper

Completion & Construction Time
2017 - 1 month

Client
Mark Turner

GFA
18.6 m^2

Design Task
Design an off grid cabin that can be flat packed and shipped to a steep mountain site

Photographer
GreenSpur/Mitch Allen

The Lost Whiskey Project is about exploring our personal limits of slowing down and simplifying. It's about the value of time and experiences over information and accumulation. This 18 square meters all- concrete structure is one part Scandinavian minimalism and two parts Virginia countryside. With a crackling fire that heats the hot tub, solar panels, cisterns, a murphy bed, a shower, and a compost toilet, this off-grid structure is virtually maintenance-free. But, the secret ingredient is the ability to escape; the trees, a warm blanket, a good book, hopefully a good drink, and with any luck, good conversation with a friend or family member. It aims to bring out the best versions of ourselves. Who we are after some quality time on the mountain, away from technology – if only for a few days. This project is about rediscovering the lost art of gathering, shelter, and nature.

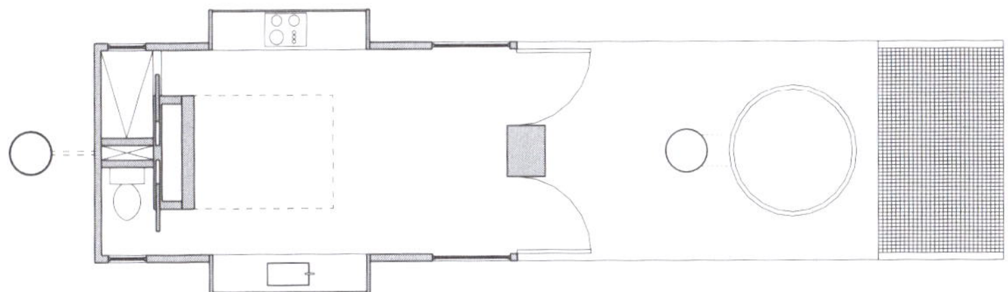

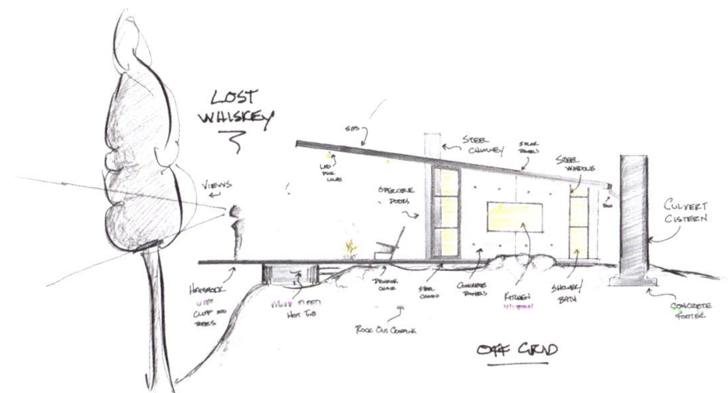

Maidla Nature Villa KASEKE

Rapla County, Estonia

Design
Mari Hunt / MARIHUNT Architects

Completion & Construction Time
2020 - 12 months

Client
Maidla Nature Resort

GFA
28 m^2

Design Task
Estonian micro-cabin standing one meter above the ground on the edge of a bog

Photographer
Priidu Saart, Tõnu Tunnel, Geete Talas

Nestled between birch trees on the edge of a bog, this building hovers one meter above the ground and is easy to reach via a wooden walkway, even during high water. The entire house is surrounded by terraces – a morning terrace at the bottom, a staircase leading to the roof, and the night terrace at the height of the treetops to watch the sunset and the stars. The sharp angles of the building's triangular shapes blend in with the surrounding bog woodland thanks to the brown ash walls. The panoramic view from the triangular bedroom faces the untamed nature. The fireplace forms the focal point, and the room can be flexibly subdivided with curtains to turn it into a bedroom and a separate workspace or rest area.

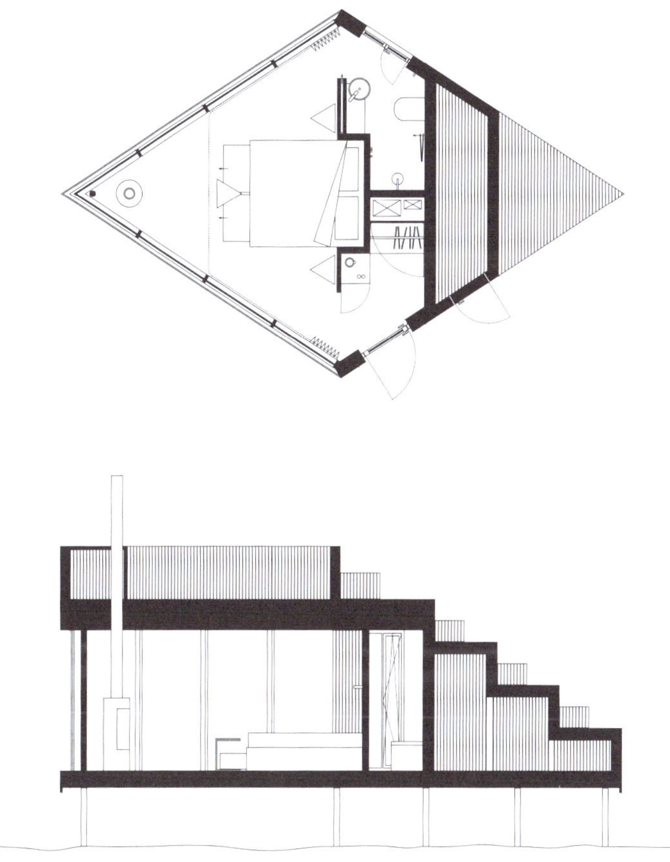

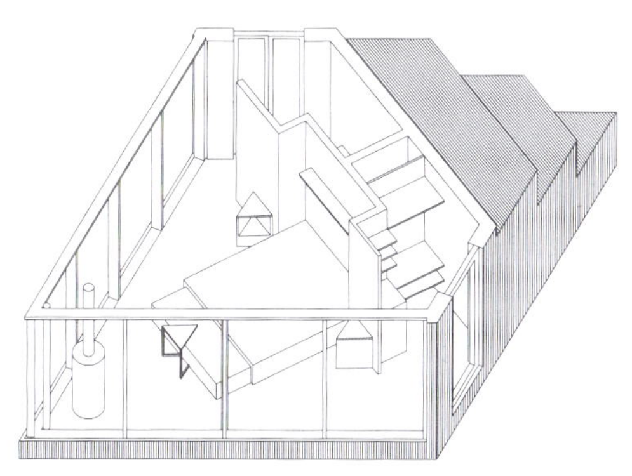

3x3 Retreat

La Unión, Chile

Design
Estudio Diagonal Architects

Completion & Construction Time
2020 - 6 months

Client
Privat

GFA
15 m^2

Design Task
A comfortable resting place in dialogue with the natural surroundings

Photographer
Estudio Diagonal Architects and Nicolás Saieh

This retreat is characterized by the tension between radical geometry and organic forest shapes. The terrace features the same footprint as the cabin and unites the spatial feeling of the outside and inside. The first floor, or "daytime story", serves as the kitchen, dining room, and living room. Here, you can spend your days by the wood-fired oven, taking in the view offered by the two-story window façade. The second, private floor accommodates the bedroom and bathroom. An area of just 15 square meters and a height of 2.4 meters on each story results in a dominant vertical spatial feeling. In contrast to the dark zinc façade, the interior cladding consists of light-colored plywood, with the house's structure consciously remaining visible.

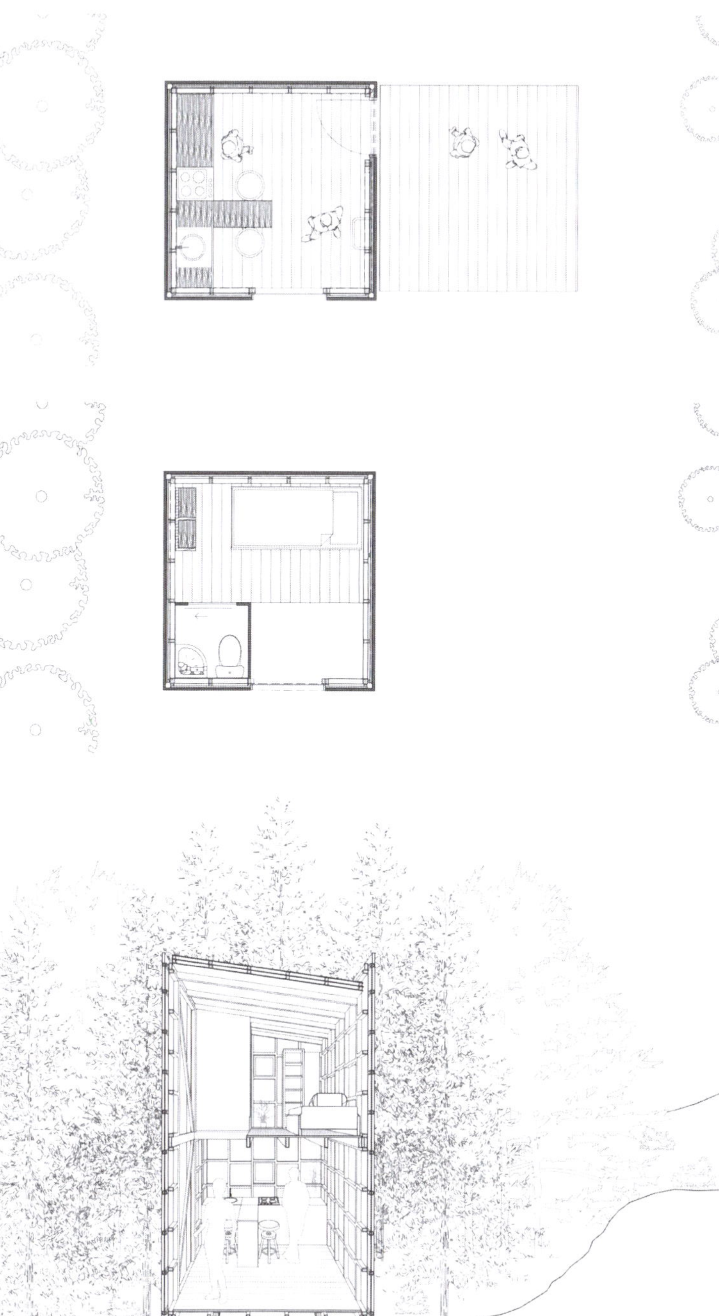

Villa Minimale

Vienna, Austria

Design
Kirsch ZT

Completion & Construction Time
2023 - 12 months

Client
Privat

GFA
50 m^2

Design Task
Allotment garden house

Photographer
Hertha Hurnaus

An allotment hut in the hills of Vienna. A retreat for relaxing, socializing, and gardening. The ground floor features a central dining area, kitchen, bathroom, toilet, and snug. The top floor accommodates three sleeping bunks with a view of the starry sky. Four identical wooden boxes have been arranged in a windmill shape, with in a central, circular oculus in the middle. The house is a prefabricated timber construction with light varnished wooden slats and a copper roof on the outside, complemented by veneered wood core plywood made of maritime pine on the inside. The relationship between the inside and outside is essential to the room atmosphere: the landscape flows through the building and offers vistas in all directions.

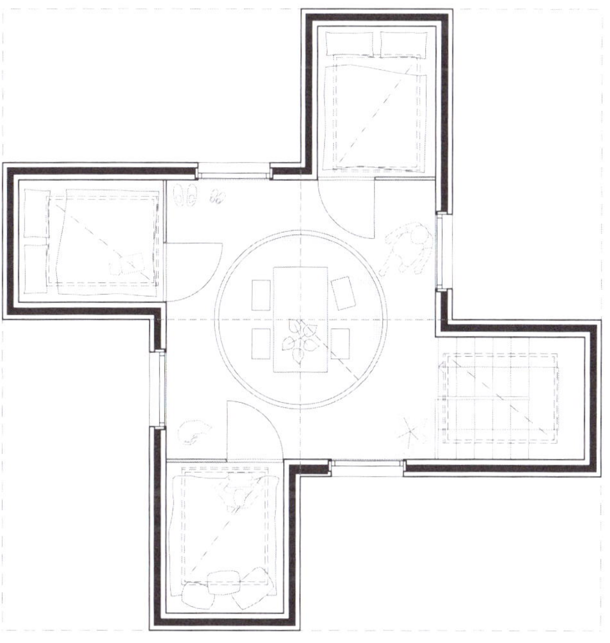

Galpão

Canela, Brazil

Design
sauermartins

Completion & Construction Time
2021 - 4 months

Client
Privat

GFA
25 m^2

Design Task
Interaction between contemporary architecture and craft practices

Photographer
Pedro Kok

The little wooden shed exhibits interactions between contemporary architecture and craft practices, which are based on the use of local construction techniques and materials. The small building was designed as an annex to the existing home and is both surrounded and concealed by vegetation. The space accommodates a studio area along with a small storage space and a firewood shelf. The external polycarbonate tiles form a light-permeable layer that guides natural light into the inner space, creating a sense of translucency and bringing playful plant shadows into the small room.

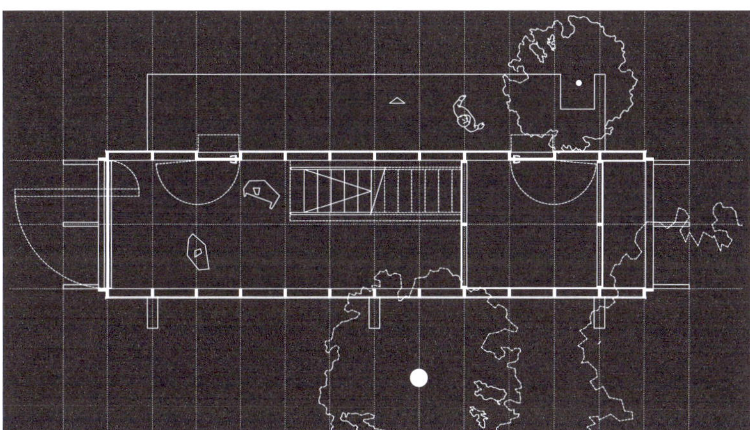

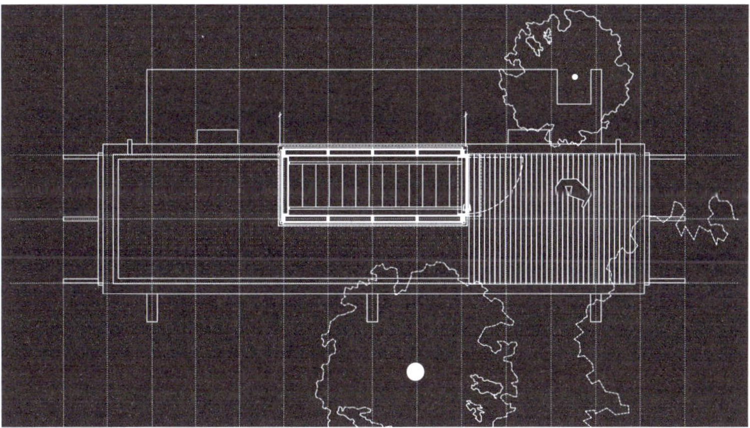

Woodnest

Odda, Norway

Design
Helen & Hard

Completion & Construction Time
Woodnest I 2020 - 8 months
Woodnest II 2023 - 10 months

Client
Sally & Kjartan Aano, Woodnest

GFA
15 m^2 each

Design Task
Four tree houses to dwell in nature

Photographer
Helen & Hard / Sindre Ellingsen

The architecture provides a concrete answer to the topography and the conditions of the location itself. Inseparably connected with nature, each tree house hangs five-six meters above the forest floor, attached to the trunk of a living pine tree with a steel collar. The interior measures just 15 square meters and features four sleeping spaces, a bathroom, a kitchen, and a living area arranged around the tree trunk in the center. From here, you can take in the far-reaching view through the trees and out to the fjord and the mountains. The architecture of each of the four tree houses aims to provide a space to take a break and appreciate the little details of the natural surroundings in which we live: the texture of the wood, the forest's daily rhythm, and the sense of living in nature.

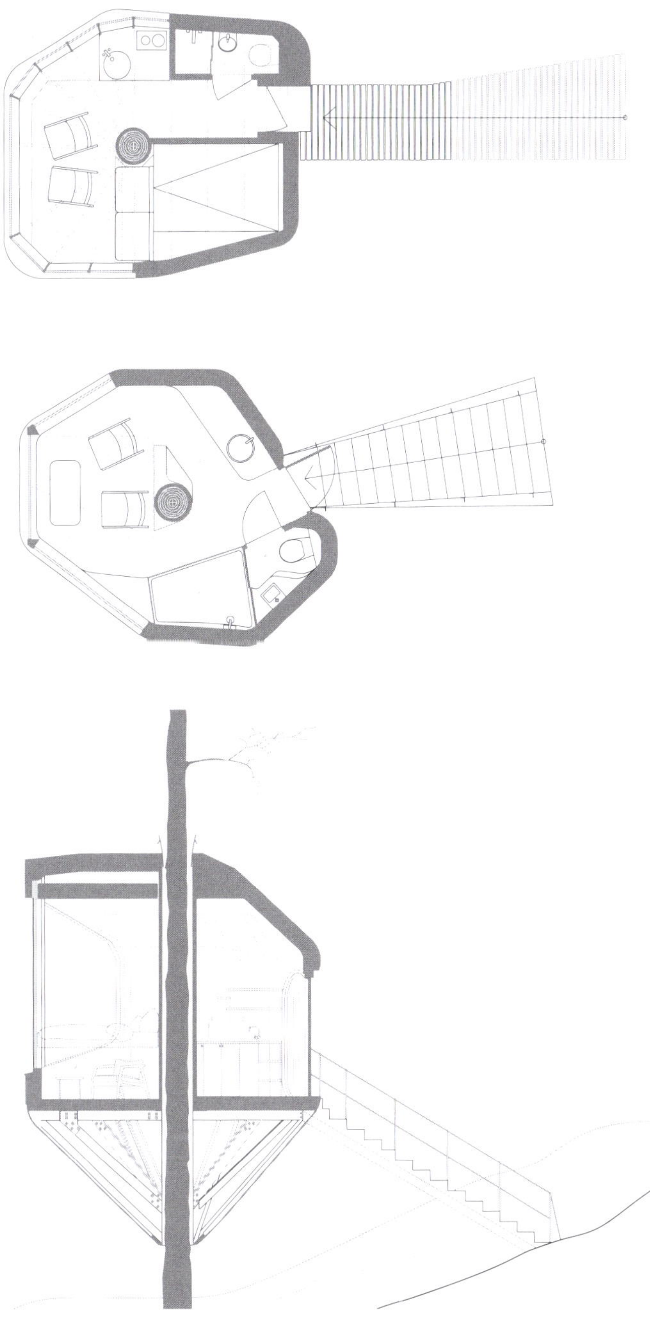

Looking Glass Lodge

East Sussex, UK

Design
Michael Kendrick Architects

Completion & Construction Time
2022 - 12 months

Client
Looking Glass Lodge Ltd

GFA
49.5 m^2

Design Task
Hybrid steel/timber structure with low impact approach

Photographer
Tom Bird

Looking Glass Lodge seamlessly blends into the High Weald Area of Outstanding Natural Beauty. The building consists of a hybrid steel/wood-frame structure with screw-pile foundations, aiming for an environmentally friendly approach. The design provides an answer to the sloping terrain and appears to sit at an elevated position between the trees, with the ground falling away below it. Red-cedar wood was chosen as a natural material for the interior and exterior cladding. Large windows flood the lodge with light and offer a sense of transparency along with far-reaching views into the woods. Self-tinting electrochromic glass ensures privacy while also preventing overheating and the emission of artificial light. Custom birch-plywood fittings subdivide the open-plan layout and separate the compact kitchen from the bedroom and en-suite bathroom.

PolyRoom

Paris, France

Design
Cutwork Studio

Completion & Construction Time
2022 - 3 months

Client
Bouygues Immobilier

GFA
25 m^2

Design Task
Single studio unit with custom furniture, prefab architecture

Photographer
Pierre CHATEL-INNOCENTI

PolyRoom is a prefabricated modular construction unit. The project aims to address today's most important urban challenges: How can design meet our growing requirement for less space? How can we use new construction methods to cover the critical need for living space? What does the modern-day home look like? The result is a prototype of a single studio unit that can be redesigned for various purposes within the compact space. Inspired by the Japanese concept of "washitsu", the design lets the bed disappear into the ceiling and transforms the bedroom into a space for various activities. The kitchen and dining area are equipped with hidden and practical features, whereas vertical storage solutions and modular accessories increase functionality.

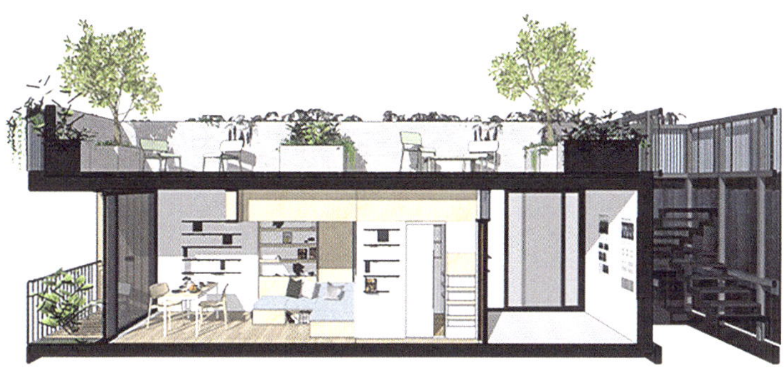

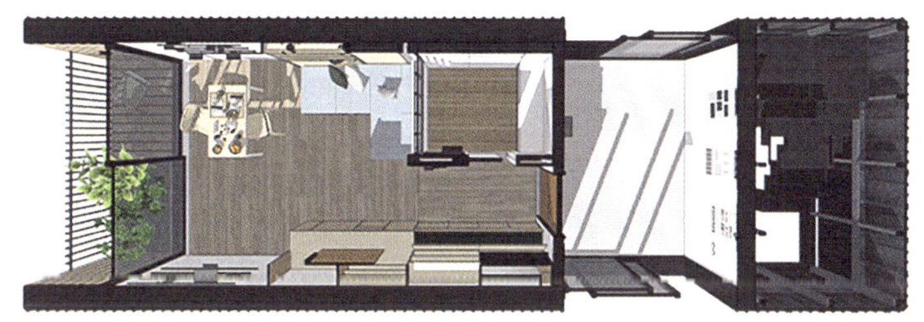

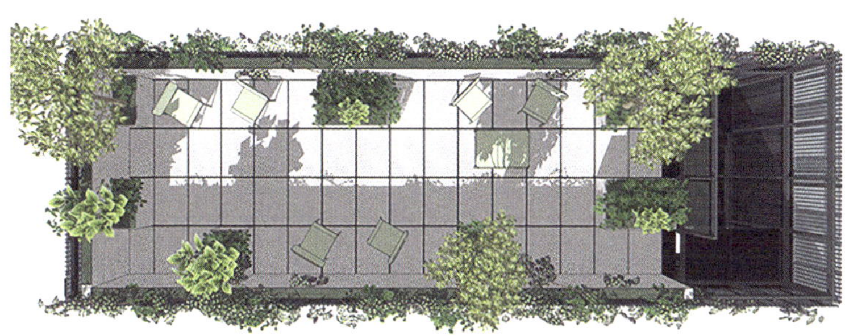

Russian Quintes-sential

Nikola-Lenivets Art Park, Russia

Design
Sergey Kuznetsov

Further participants
KROST, CPU Pride

Completion & Construction
2021 - 12 months

Client
Nikola-Lenivets, art park

GFA
36 m^2

Design Task
Pipe-shaped art object

Photographer
Rustam Shagimardanov

The Russian Quintessential house is an art object in the shape of a pipe, with a diameter of 3.5 meters and a length of 12 meters. Due to its placement on the terrain, the structure is literally hanging in the air. The creators employed complex engineering techniques normally used in shipbuilding to construct the building. The result is a building frame formed out of supporting ribs, like the body of a ship, and its impressive weight of around 12 tons is balanced on only six bolts. The building provides all modern amenities. Its residents can live in it, stay the night, cook, and shower. The interior features a modern style with wood and metal.

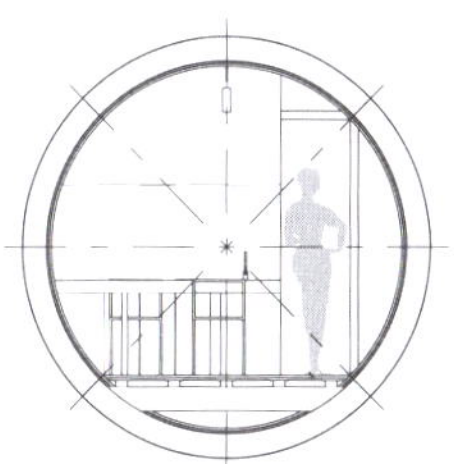

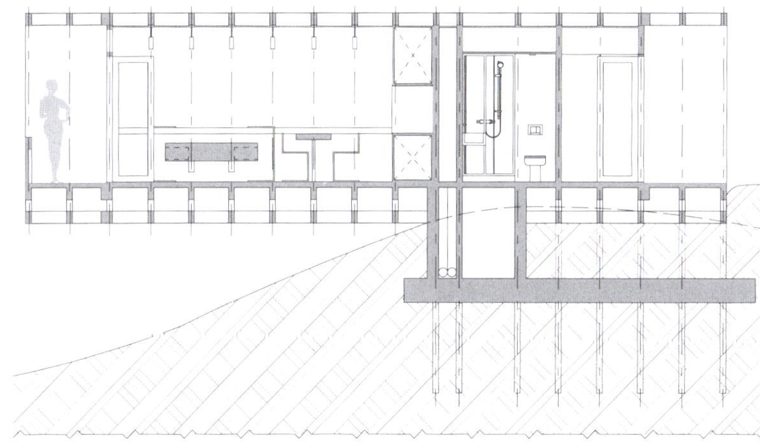

Majamaja Village Helsinki

Helsinki, Finland

Design
Littow architectes

Completion & Construction Time
2023 - 12 months

Client
Majamaja Oy

GFA
23 m^2 per cabin

Design Task
Off-grid cabins with timeless aesthetic

Photographer
Chikako Harada, Joonas Linkola
and Pekka Littow

The project is inspired by the life of the Finnish archipelagos: traditional housing, human-scale buildings, and a lifestyle in which humans live in harmony with nature. The huts unite timeless aesthetic with modern design. Optimized through storage space integrated into the floor thickness and foldable furniture, the living space allows for multiple uses. The construction materials consist almost entirely of solid wood. The surfaces are minimalist and refined to create a calm ambiance. The units comprise prefabricated elements that can be assembled without heavy construction machinery. This makes the installation easy, even in remote locations. Several units can be combined to create larger complexes.

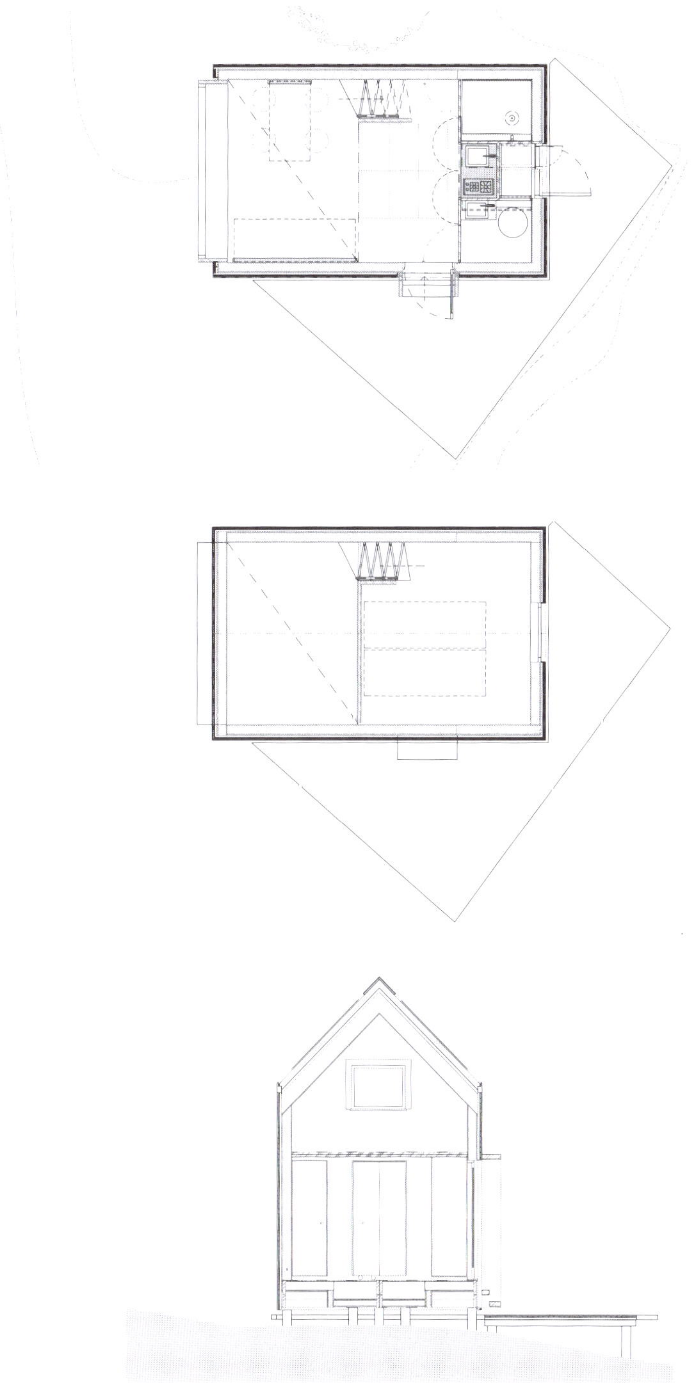

Cabin 192

Altos del María, Panama

Design
Isturaín+Sam Architecture

Completion & Construction Time
2018 - 12 months

Client
Private

GFA
36 m^2

Design Task
Cabin hut based on the principles of tropical architecture

Photographer
Alfredo Martiz and Nadine Sam

Cabin 192 is a family project situated in Altos del María, a hilly area in western Panama. The ground and top floors measure about 60 square meters in total. A footbridge leads into the living space, which accommodates a bathroom, bedroom and a kitchenette. Adapted to the tropical climate, the construction floats above ground level to avoid excess humidity. Carefully positioned windows ensure temperature balance and good ventilation. Local construction workers implemented this project together with the family.

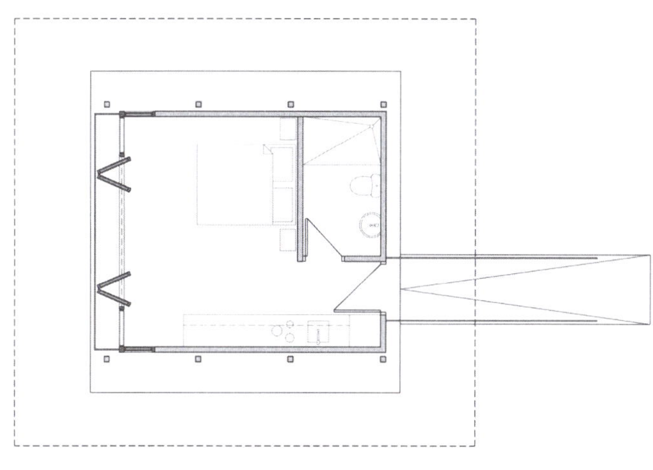

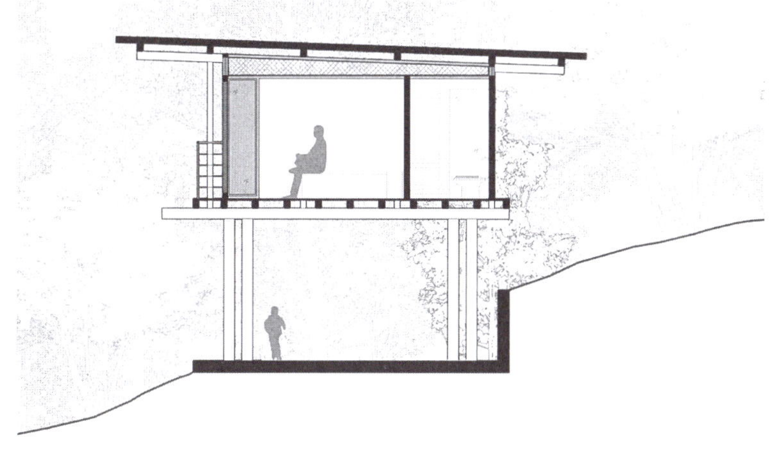

SHELTER

Vyšný Medzev, Slovakia

Design
GRAU architects

Completion & Construction Time
2022 - 2 months

Client
Košice Self-Govering Region,
Košice region of turism, Hikemates

GFA
30 m^2

Design Task
Wooden refuge surrounded by nature
to contribute to national tourism

Photographer
Matej Hakár

Situated on a hiking trail at an elevation of 850 meters, this shelter serves as a refuge for hikers and a year-round meeting place for outdoor fanatics. The inner space is very functional and does without any unnecessary elements to ensure optimal comfort for the hut's purpose. The house's entire structure consists of wood, with plywood panels and beams forming the frame. The interior is clad with stained and lacquered plywood, while the exterior dons black-stained spruce boards. This minimalist approach results in comfortable and durable accommodation that blends into the natural surroundings.

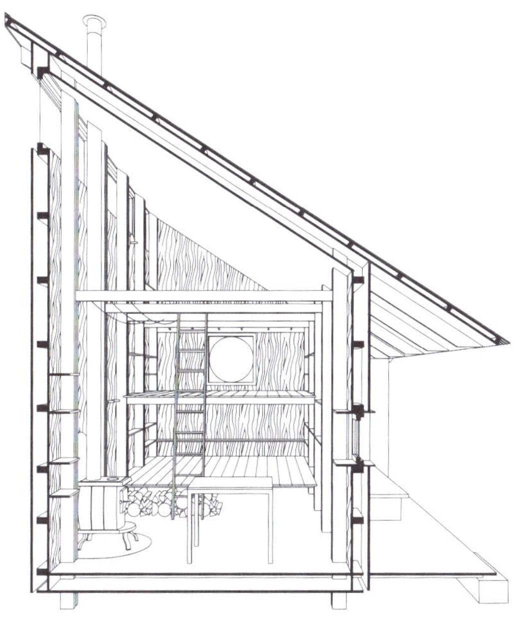

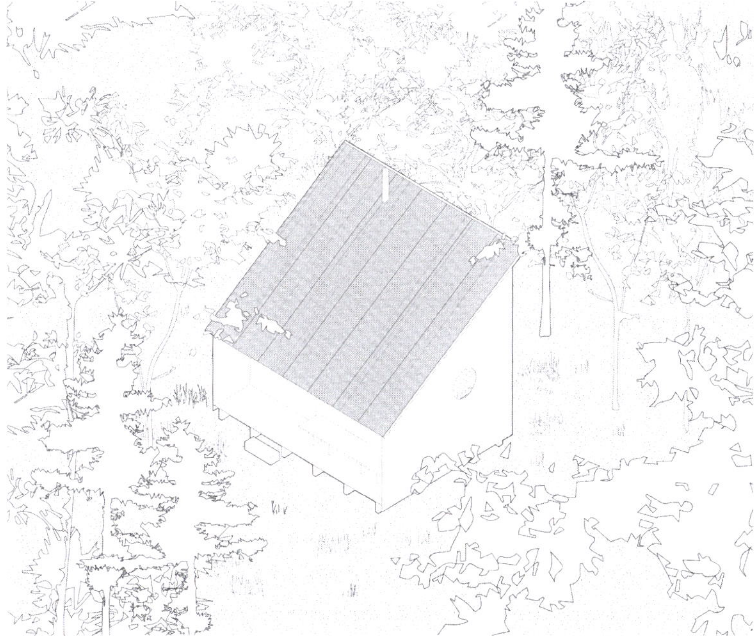

Mezzanina Cabin

Valdivia, Chile

Design
Arce&Westermeier Architects

Completion & Construction Time
2022 - 12 months

Client
Rodrigo Vasquez

GFA
45 m^2

Design Task
Small cabin set in a sloping area of the property adjacent to the main house

Photographer
Nicolas Saieh

Mezzanina Cabin gently slots into the sloping part of the property, while the piles on which it stands give it some height. It opens up towards the west with a fully glazed, nearly six-meter-long façade, revealing breathtaking views. On the rear entry side, the façade appears closed, homogenous, and dark, with the exception of a few openings. The sloped roof is a response to the heavy local rainfall. The very generous living room stretches across the entire breadth of the house and accommodates the kitchen, living, and sleeping areas. A cleverly integrated mezzanine floor adds a private retreat to the living space.

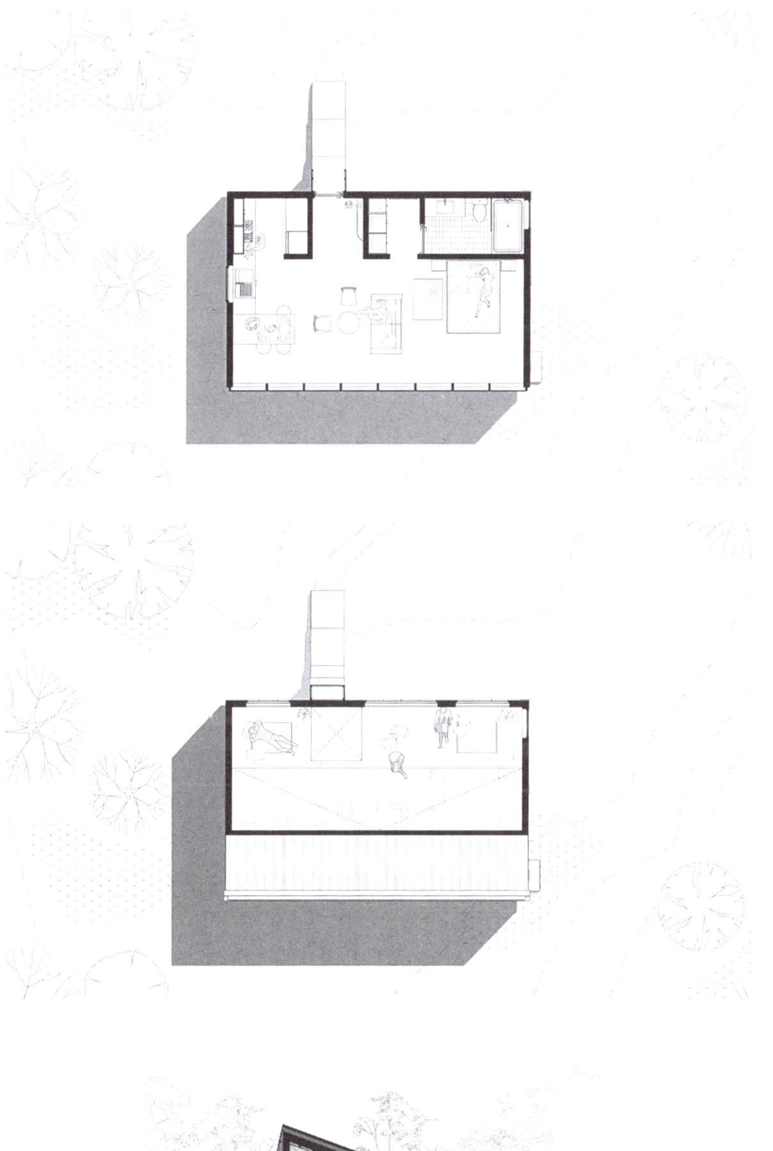

LOVE2 HOUSE

Tokyo, Japan

Design
Takeshi Hosaka / Takeshi Hosaka Architects

Completion & Construction Time
2019 - 26 months

Client
Takeshi & Megumi Hosaka

GFA
18.84 m^2

Design Task
A one-storey house created by fighting the "infinity of small things" in a logical and sensual way

Photographer
Nacasa & Partners Inc.

LOVE2 HOUSE is a one-storey house that spans just 18.84 square meters but still accommodates all living areas. In winter, the two skylights gently illuminate the house, while flooding the space with sunlight in the summer. The roof consists of two shells that connect at varying heights and form a simple cubage. The eaves of the roof shells are straight, blending in with the environment, while the top part is slightly bent. Seven short walls separate the three areas: dining room, kitchen, and bedroom. The thickness of the walls is tapered from top to bottom to allow for built-in shelves and the kitchen counter.

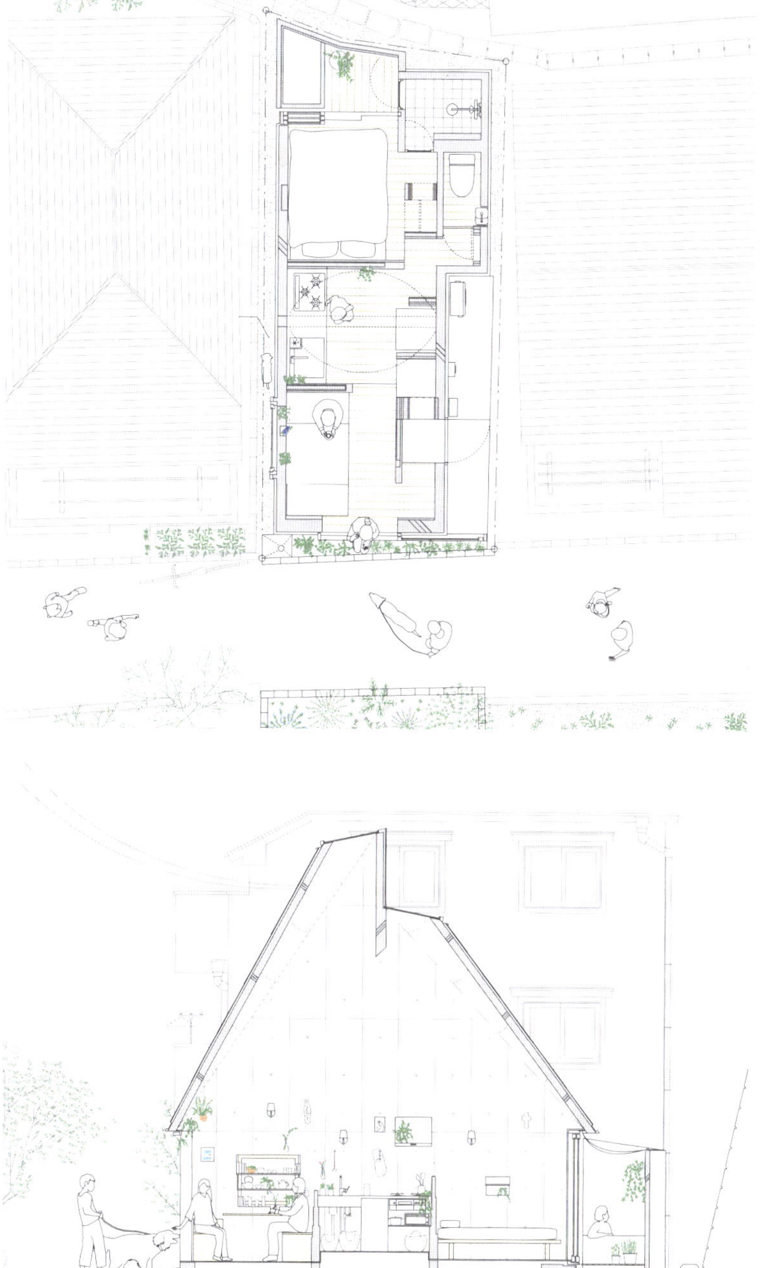

H-EVA

Ustaritz, France

Design
A6A

Builder
My Little Loft

Completion & Construction Time
2018 - 12 months

Client
Private

GFA
20 m^2

Design Task
Prefabricated, transportable
and autonomous

Photographer
Agnès Clotis

H-EVA is a space experience that opens up towards the landscape and is aware of our everyday needs. Prefabricated, transportable and autonomous to differing degrees. It draws from elements of nature – sun, water, and wood, which is its sole construction material. After leaving the workshop, H-EVA is transported to its destination with a flatbed truck and installed with a crane. Depending on its use and application, the house is available in three different widths: 2.50 m, 3 m and 3.50 m. The length of the modules can vary between 8, 9 and 12 m. The maximum height is 3.40 m. It is possible to combine the elements to create larger units.

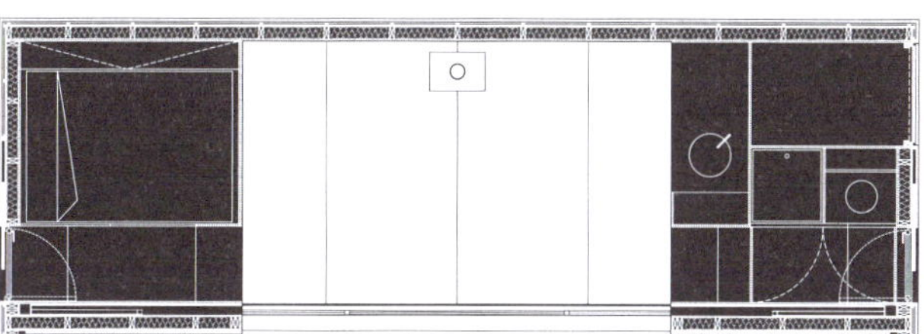

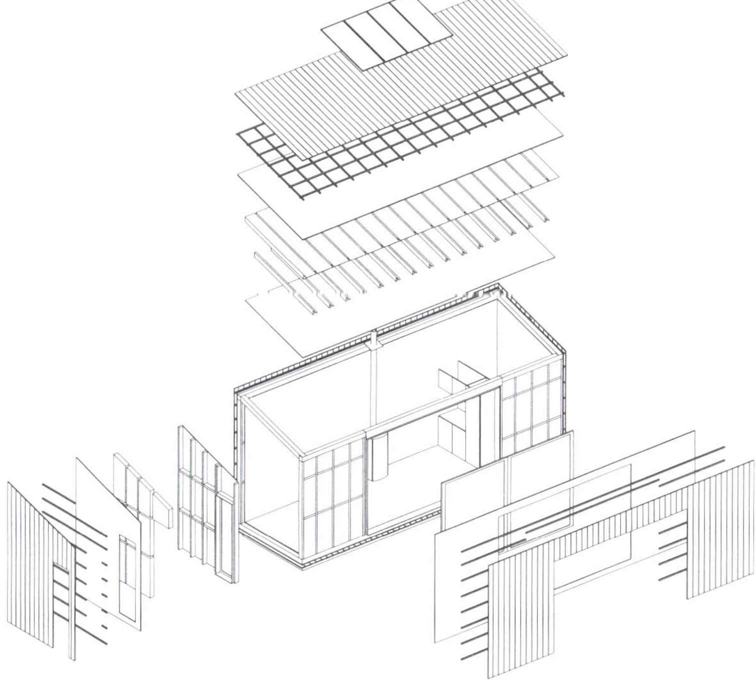

House on 12 Legs

Zebegény, Hungary

Design
RJZS Architects

Completion & Construction Time
2020 - 12 months

Client
Private

GFA
30 m^2

Design Task
Treehouse

Photographer
Balázs Danyi

The House on 12 Legs, a vacation home made of a light wood structure, is located in Zebegény, Hungary. It stands in a dense forest with particularly steep terrain. The gable-roofed house, opening on its shorter side, faces the Danube and interferes as little as possible with the beautiful surroundings. The entrance to the building lies directly at the top end of the stairs, without any further elevation. It leads to the elongated main room, which brings you to the terrace that offers a spectacular view over the treetops and the impressive riverbend.

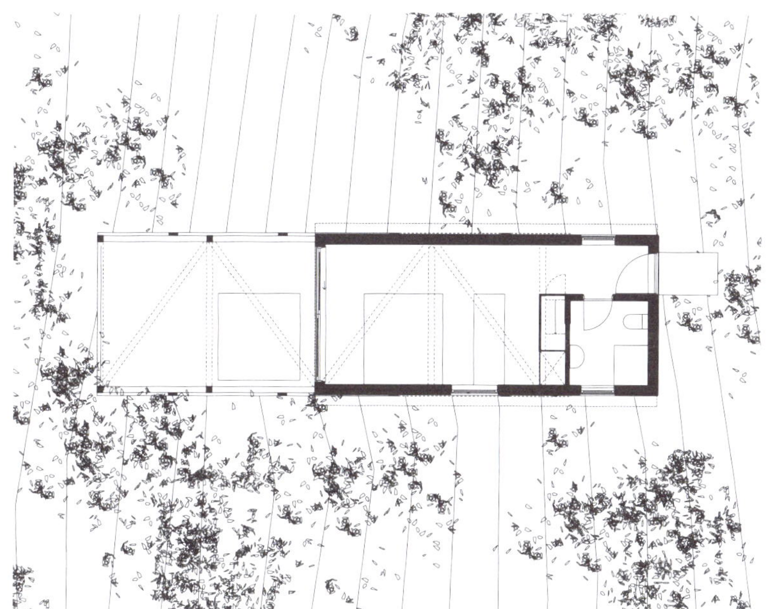

Atelier

Kysuce, Slovakia

Design
ARK - Shelter

Completion & Construction Time
2021 - prefabrication 3 months, on site 5 days

Client
Martin Mikov□ák

GFA
37 m^2 per module

Design Task
Open plan

Photographer
Peter Fabo

A space for living, creating, and meditating. Compact from the outside, partly sunk into the ground to merge with the fields, and partially hovering above the valley to disconnect. The space consists of three connected modules, with a fireplace serving as a central hub between them that provides warmth and orientation. The remaining space spreads out centrifugally. Life starts with an entry hall facing southeast, providing access to the open south-west-north platform of the day zone. After rising from a restorative sleep at dawn, the space guides you towards the sunrise through the washing area and back to the entrance to close the circle of this form of therapy.

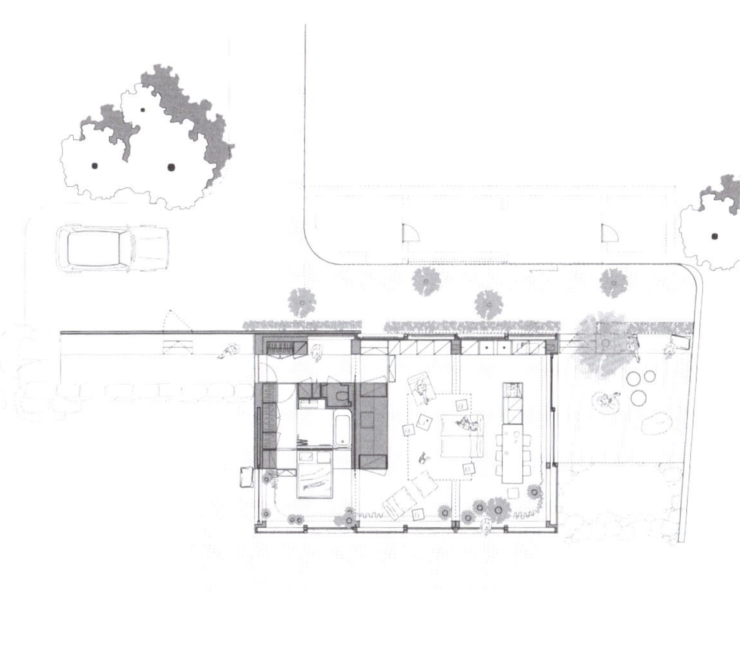

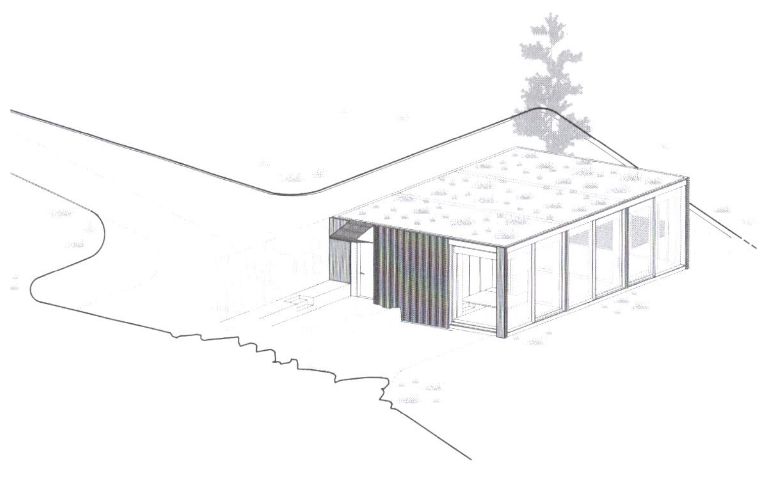

Klein Cabin

Bethel Woods, USA

Design
BIG - Bjarke Ingels Group

Completion & Construction Time
2018 - 24 months

Client
Klein House

GFA
17 m^2

Design Task
A building scaled down to a product, sized to be delivered on site in modules made of recyclable materials

Photographer
Anton Bak, Matthew Carbone and Thomas Loof

Klein Cabin is delivered in modules consisting entirely of recyclable materials. Generous, frameless windows and a canvas stretch across the structure, creating a seamless, weather-proof cover. The free-standing wooden frame and the dark insulating cork bring nature indoors. A small fireplace is tucked away in one corner, while off-grid equipment is stored in the back of the house, resulting in a reliable and self-powered house. Klein Cabin's crystal-like shape lends the hut a constantly evolving appearance – changing perspectives turn it into a simple cube, a tapered tower, or create a classic A-frame silhouette.

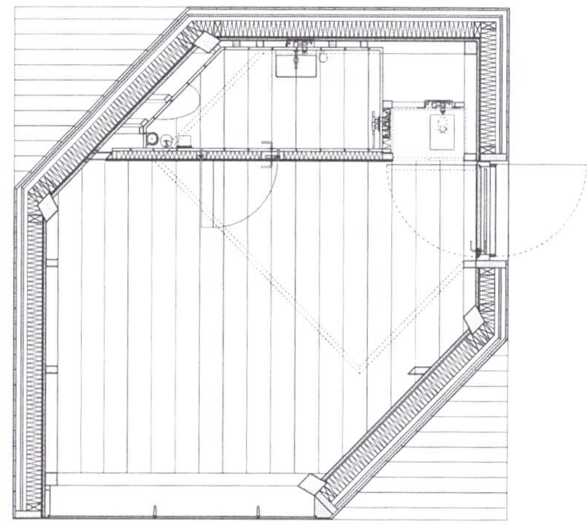

Glasan

Isle of Skye, Scotland

Design
Dualchas Architects

Completion & Construction Time
2024 - 12 months

Client
Laura + Neil Stephen

GFA
45 m^2

Design Task
A simple form in an open landscape with a rich and quirky interior

Photographer
Richard Gaston

Glasan, Gaelic for "gray object", contains just 45 square meters of interior space and features a recessed bed in the main living area, inspired by the traditional "box bed" once common in Hebridean huts. The house aims to provide visitors with a special experience of Skye's landscape from within a unique work of architecture. The simple timber-framed construction sits on an elevated steel platform. The walls are insulated with sheep's wool and most of the windows are small. However, one large window to the gable opens completely, sliding into a pocket behind the cladding, which allows guests to sit on the window cill and take in the sea air and the view of the extensive beach along with the Cuillin mountains beyond.

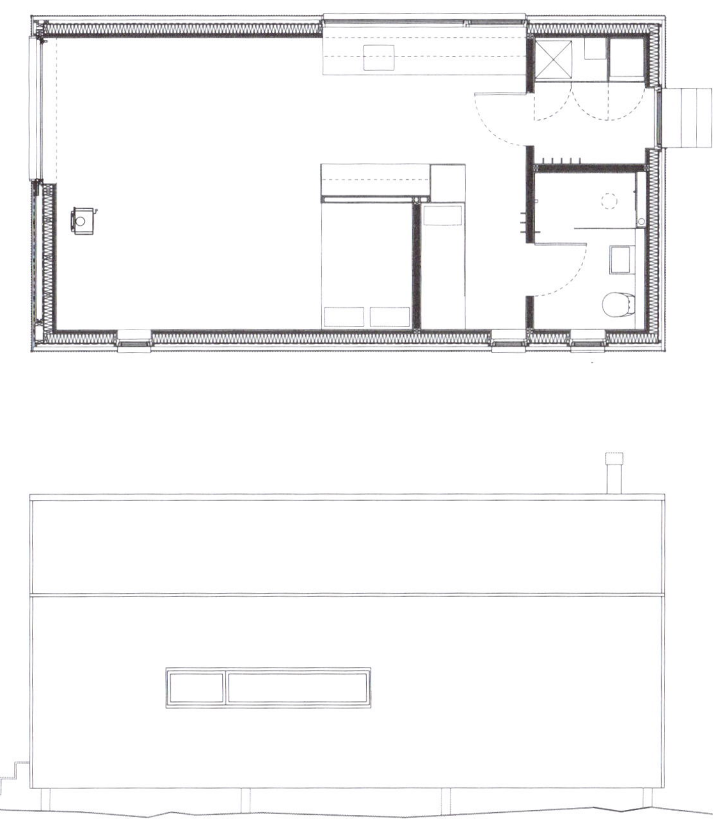

O'CASELLA

Sari-Solenzara, France

Design
Atelier LAVIT

Further participants
Architecture Nature

Completion & Construction Time
2022 - 2 months

Client
Private

GFA
13 m^2

Design Task
Prefabricated wooden modular cabin

Photographer
Atelier LAVIT

O'CASELLA is a modular prefabricated housing system consisting of two elements: a living module and a pergola. The living module includes a utility room, a kitchen, and a living and sleeping area with a view of the surrounding nature. The pergola is a ventilated and shady structure that creates an outdoor space for thinking, reading, and relaxing. "Laricciu" wood, which is particularly durable, was used for the external cladding and the structure. Inside, the walls and the ceiling are covered in MDF wood. The façade's striking steel rail emphasizes the horizontality of the entire volume and serves as rain gutter as well as a guide for moving the façade panel.

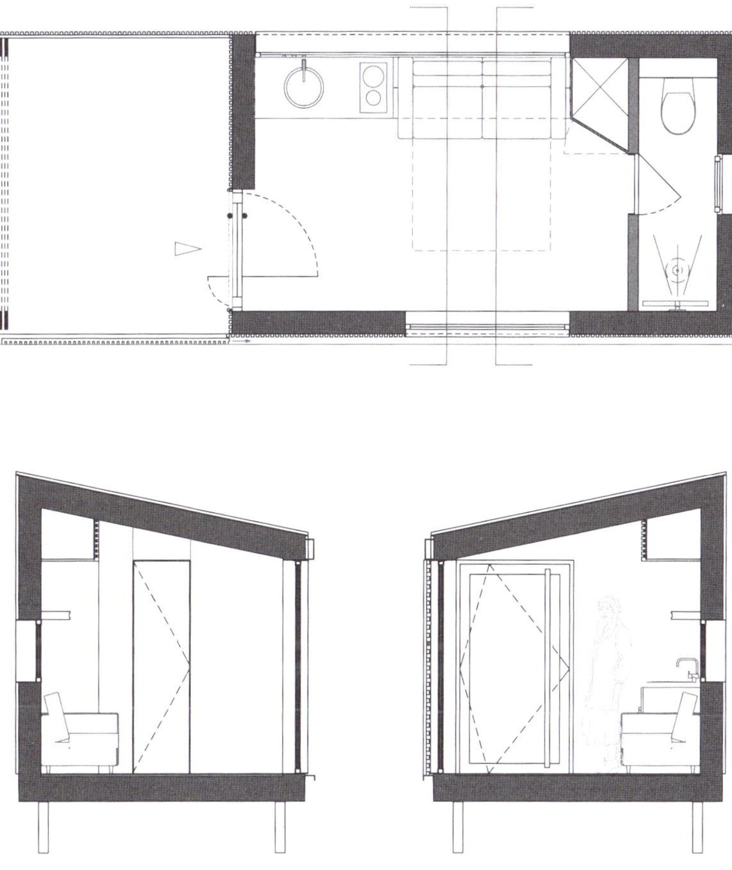

Oasis

Santa Monica, USA

Design
Minarc

Further participants
Erla Construction

Completion & Construction Time
2019 - 5 months

Client
Michael Solomon

GFA
32.5 m^2

Design Task
Energy-efficient solutions in
a modern tiny house

Photographer
Art Gray Photography

This state-of-the-art house unites style, efficiency, and sustainability on a footprint of just 35 square meters. Sleek lines, innovative materials, and intelligent technologies optimize the use of space, while the well-thought-out layout offers a smart combination of functionality and aesthetics. From the cozy living area and the space-saving kitchenette through to the cutting-edge bathroom, every inch has been designed with care to meet the demands of modern living. Solar panels and rain-water usage give the dwelling an environmentally friendly footprint. Oasis is built with mnmMOD, a building system that does not support fire.

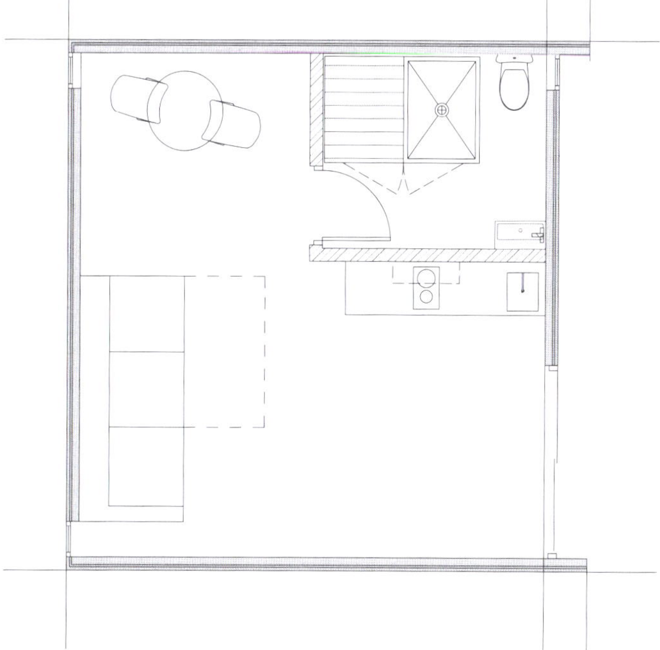

Terra Tiny Houses

Alentejo, Portugal

Design
Madeiguincho

Completion & Construction Time
2024 - 12 months

Client
Privat

GFA
13 m^2 x 3

Design Task
Three tiny houses for a regenerative agriculture farm at Alqueva

Photographer
João Carranca

In contrast to conventional residential construction, the architects pursued the goal of creating a living object in which the residents experience and inhabit the space on different levels, contributing to a more organic and unique lifestyle. The living area was maximized and opened up through the design of compact and efficient kitchen and bathroom spaces. Every house comes with an observatory terrace. Consistent finishes and materials establish a connection between the three houses, with façades covered in cork rind – not only reminiscent of the cork oaks in the surrounding forests, but also improving insulation.

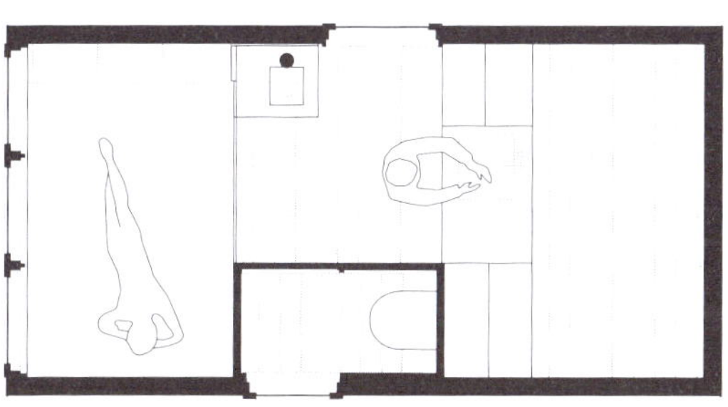

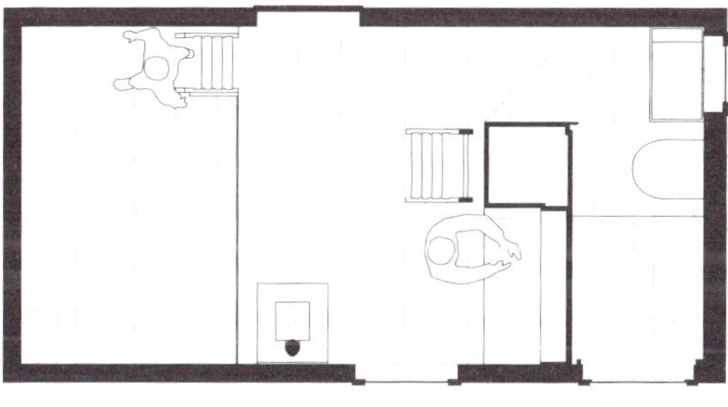

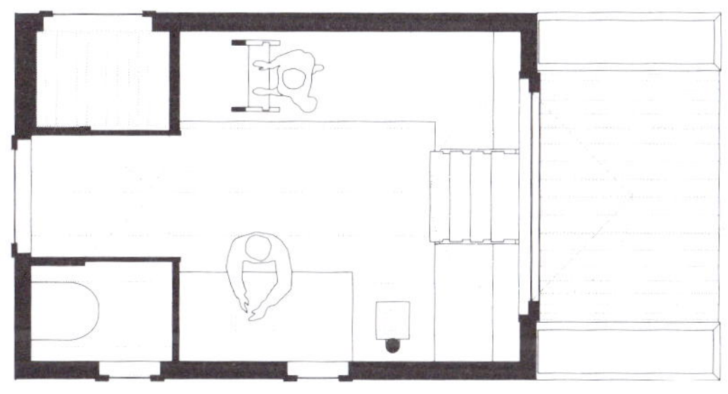

Altar Ninho

São Paulo, Brazil

Design
Natureza Urbana

Completion & Construction Time
2023 - 6 months

Client
Altar

GFA
40 m^2

Design Task
Prefabrication, use of responsible attributes to maximise the nature immersion experience

Photographer
Maíra Acayaba

The design is based on the prefabrication of the house's main elements – the metal structure, the façade solutions, and the closures – all of which were transported in one trip and quickly assembled on the construction site after arrival. Standing on metal columns – which ensures minimal impact on the ground – and accompanied by a generous natural-wood deck, the 20 square metre accommodation combines a living space, kitchen and bedroom in a unique environment. In the outside area, guests can make use of a leisure area with furniture, a shower and space for a bonfire and to take in the beautiful view.

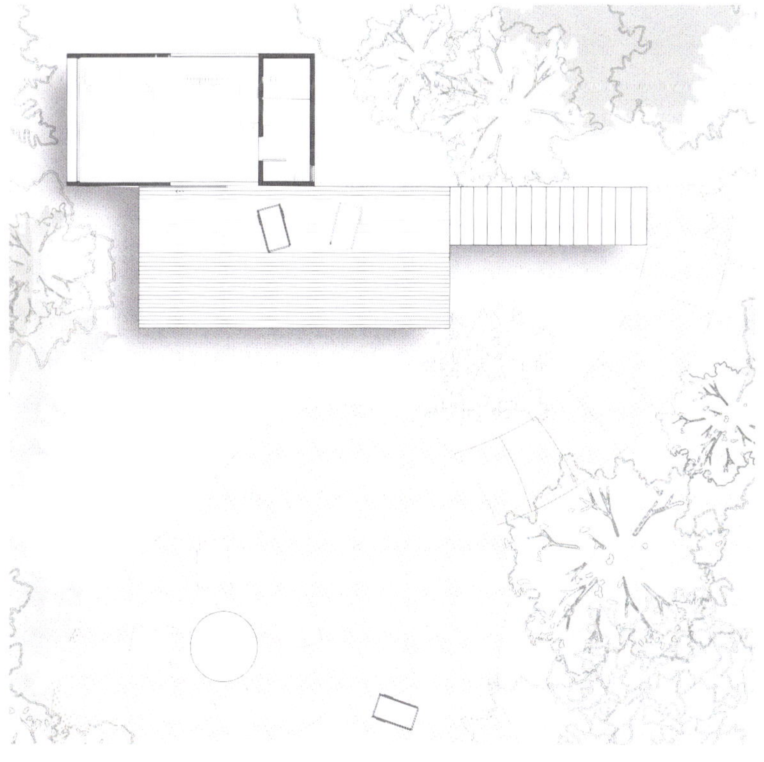

Tiny Home on the Water

Berlin, Germany

Design
Crossboundaries

Completion & Construction Time
2022 - 16 months

Client
Marianne Friese

GFA
62 m^2

Design Task
Transform a boat into a tiny home

Photographer
Johanna Link

-MF 862
BERLIN

Crossboundaries has redesigned a solar-powered motorboat, incorporating high-end tiny-home features, ideal for slow-paced travel. Measuring about 15 meters in length and four meters in width, it comprises interconnected multi-purpose areas. Key design elements include a flip-over bed that conceals the helm stand, a folding kitchen table, and a pull-out desk, making the space both practical and adaptable. This sustainable, floating tiny home represents a shift toward minimalist, flexible living, offering high-quality spaces that seamlessly adapt to modern needs.

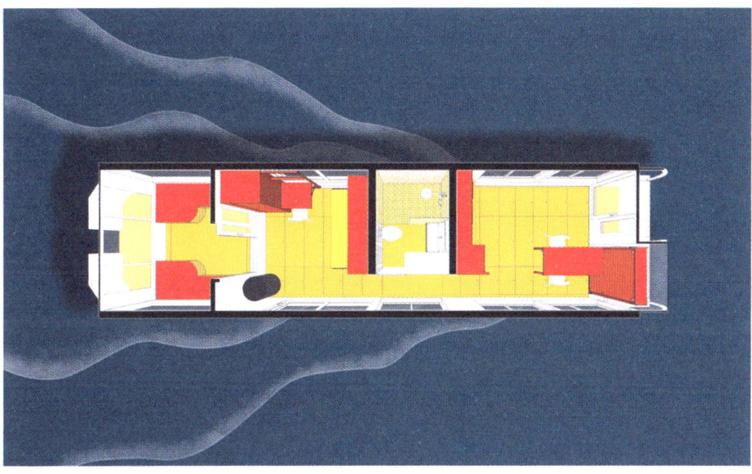

Tree Hoose

Ullapool, Scotland

Design
ECHO

Completion & Construction Time
2021 - 6 months

Client
Studiohoose.co.uk

GFA
18.5 m^2

Design Task
Prefabricated structure engineered to be airlifted to an inaccessible hillside

Photographer
Echo

The Tree Hoose hut lies on a steep lakeshore and was constructed in such a way that five prefabricated sections were delivered directly to the site by helicopter. A steel platform, anchored in the rocks of the slope, served to position the individual sections as they were lowered between the trees. The cross-shaped layout of the light-flooded living space, measuring 18.5 square meters, accommodates a bedroom, a living room, a built-in kitchen, and a shower room, arranged around the central wood burner with skylights. The interior walls and surfaces are made of timber, and the view allows the observer to immerse themselves into the birch wood. The bed sits at the same elevation as the forest floor, the glazed wall of the shower room overlooks the forest's leaf canopy. A window seat and a small balcony offer a wonderful vista of the lake and the distant mountains.

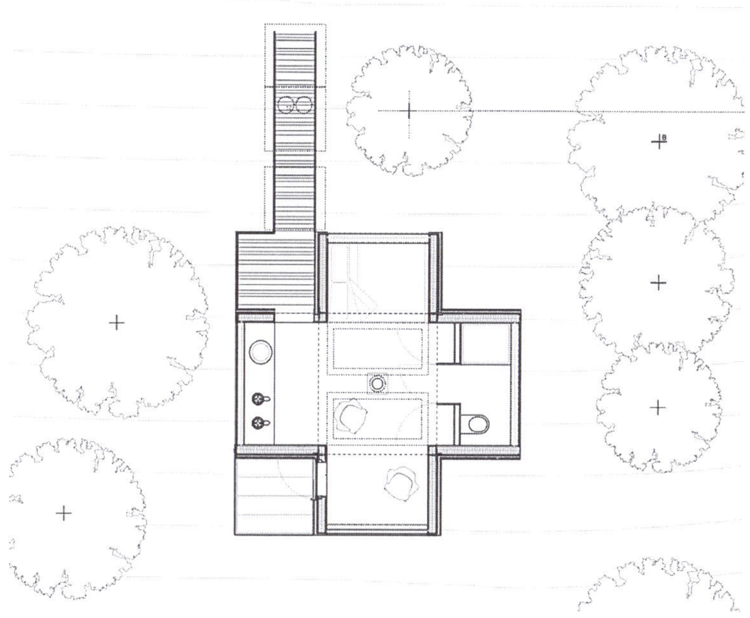

Lodging in the Quarry

Baños de Agua Santa, Ecuador

Design
La Cabina de la Curiosidad
Marie Combette and Daniel Moreno Flores

Completion & Construction Time
2022 - 4 months

Client
Alexandra Torres, Kevin Torres,
Margarita Castro and Jorge Torres

GFA
21 m^2 each lodgings
10 m^2 kitchen cabin

Design Task
Small lodges open to the surrounding nature

Photographer
Bicubik Photography and
La Cabina de la Curiosidad
Marie Combette and Daniel Moreno Flores

The two lodgings were erected in a quarry, part of which is returned to its natural state. The huge stones that act as structural supports are remnants of the old quarry. Stone slabs from a large boulder have been integrated into the cabins as sinks. Gravel and sand were taken from the nearby quarry to form the paths and outdoor facilities. Old sieves and pipelines, also from the quarry, serve as building materials for the cabins. The new pine and Colorado wood ensures quality and comfort in the cabins' interior. The large glass surfaces reveal a view of the Tungurahua volcano.

mü_see_ haus

Uferpark Überlingen, Germany

Design
Sägezahn Architektur in Holz

Completion & Construction Time
2020 - 3 months

Client
Landesgartenschau Überlingen

GFA
13 m^2

Design Task
A capsule made of wood and glass

Photographer
Nina Baisch

The goal: to build a timber house using everything a tree has to offer. The result is that 99% of the construction materials are renewable and recyclable. Developed in harmony with nature, this tiny house has a simple and attractive appearance. It highlights the surroundings and is mobile and ready to relocate anytime. Enveloped by three layers, you gaze across vast expanses of the lake. The interior layer of light wood provides a shell, the second, middle layer consisting of wood fiber insulation gives warmth, and the outer layer out of larch wood offers protection against the elements. The walls and ceilings are made of a three-layer spruce panel, the floor and window bench of ash.

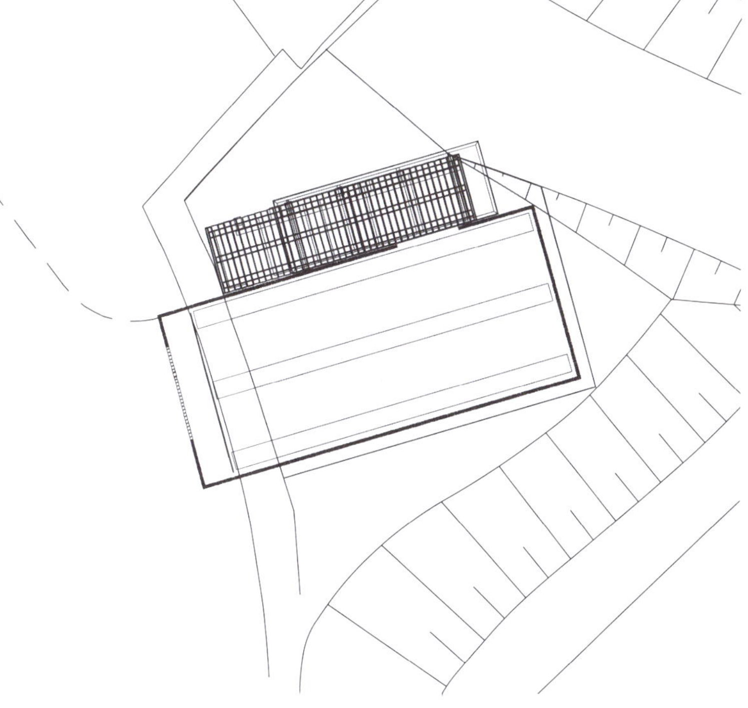

Punta Casitas Cabin 1

Boyacá, Colombia

Design
Yemail Arquitectura

Builder
ENTI.ERRA

Completion & Construction Time
2022 - 6 months

Client
Edgar A Contreras

GFA
63 m^2

Design Task
Refuge as a tribute to the surrounding nature and the communities that inhabit it

Photographer
Mateo Pérez and Edgar Contreras

Punta Casitas is situated in the rugged mountains near Lake Tota, connecting the architecture with the natural surroundings. The hut was constructed with local materials, such as yellow pinewood and dark clay tiles, and harmoniously blends into the landscape. To access the house, you climb up a path that leads to a semi-covered space on a mezzanine level, which is connected to the bathroom. From here, a passage takes you to a bathtub that is protected on both sides and focused on the distance. The lower level has integrated the social areas, including the kitchen, the dining room, and a suspended terrace. A large window acts as the key feature of the upper floor's main room, offering a vista of the lake's wonderful vastness.

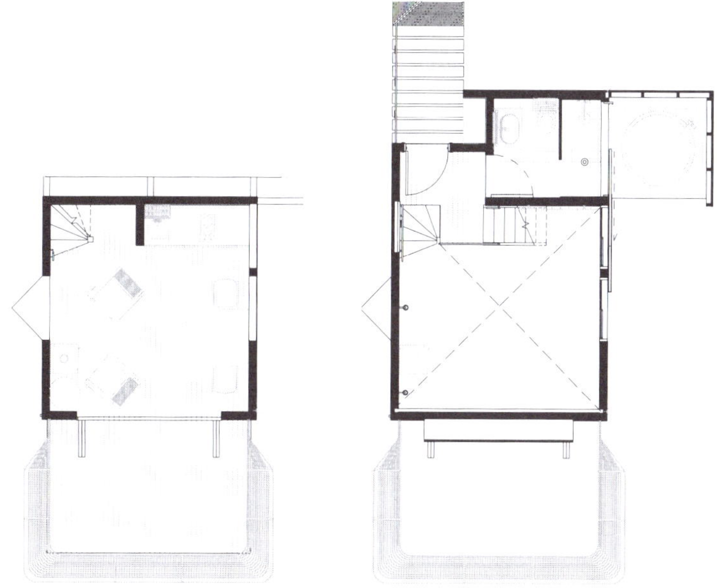

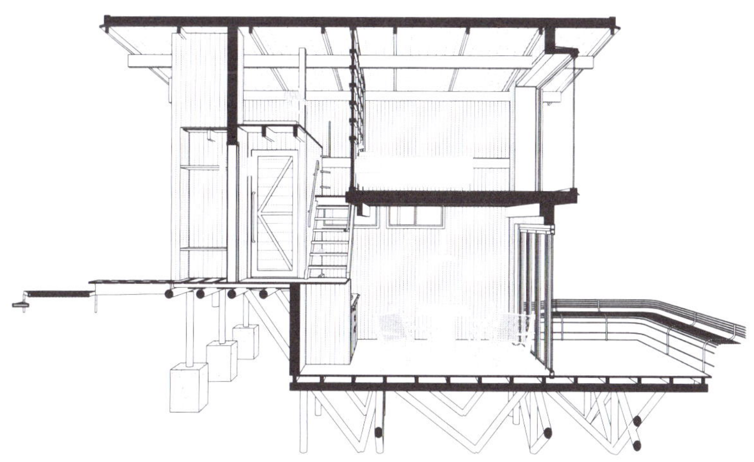

Decatur Island Bunkhouse

Decatur Island, USA

Design
The Miller Hull Partnership

Completion & Construction Time
2019 - 12 months

Client
Joel and Michelle VandenBrink,
Ken Bounds and Linda Gorton

GFA
37 m^2

Design Task
Accessory structure to existing cabin, compact layout

Photographer
Juan Benavides and
The Miller Hull Partnership

Decatur Island Bunkhouse, situated next to the Decatur Island Cabin designed by Robert Hull, follows the principle of "light on the land and no more than necessary". The bunkhouse hovers above the site, reinforcing the impression of a sloping topography. A timber exoskeleton nods to the original cabin, framing a compact, efficient interior with two sleeping areas separated by a central bathroom. Positioned for privacy and views, the design includes porches on each end—one grounded, the other cantilevered toward the water. Passive strategies like optimized orientation, roof overhangs, and clerestory windows reduce energy use and maximize natural ventilation.

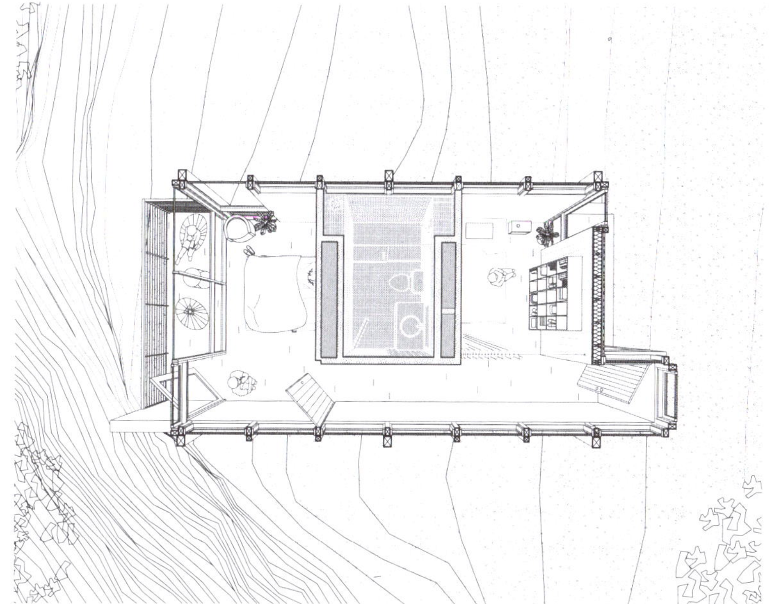

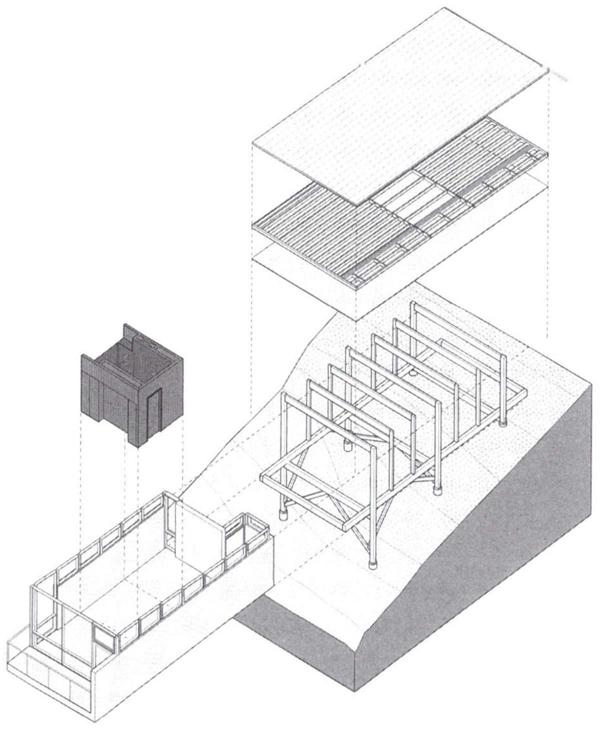

Cabin ANNA

Werkendam, The Netherlands

Design
Caspar Schols

Completion & Construction Time
2020 - 4 weeks

Client
Private

GFA
34-57 m^2

Design Task
Multi-layer cabine that can be opened and closed

Photographer
Jorrit `t Hoen

The Cabin ANNA invites visitors to connect with their surroundings and invites the outdoor environment inside. The cabin features several layers that can be opened and closed, like a piece of clothing that you can put on or take off depending on your mood and the circumstances. A special type of construction allows you to open and close the layers by hand. The cabin's outer layer looks like the classic, archetypal house we are all familiar with, but as soon as you slide it open, it takes on a completely different shape. This new shape appears more surreal and abstract and unveils the inner construction with its strong, graphic lines.

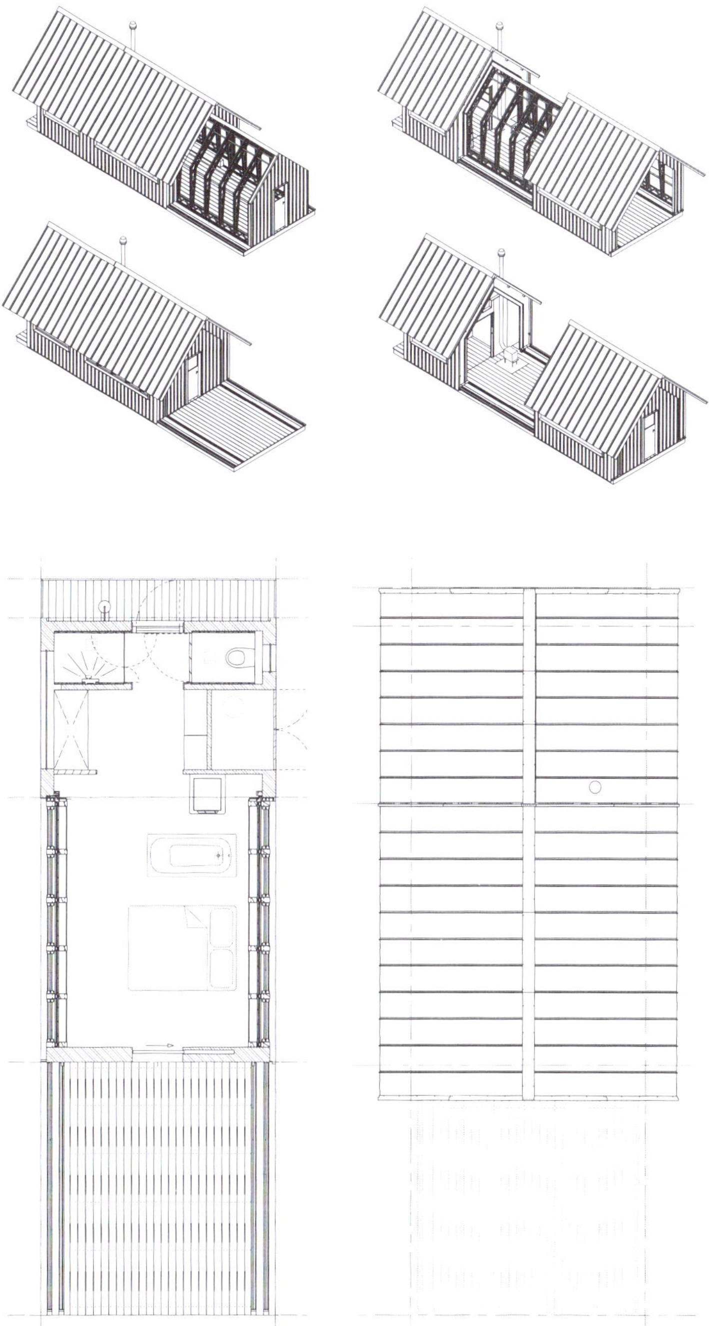

Cottage Sirákov

Liptál, Czech Republic

Design
ellement architects

Completion & Construction Time
2017 - 12 months

Client
Tomáš Novosad

GFA
30 m^2

Design Task
Wooden cottage with a compact shape

Photographer
Dušan Tománek

The building's spatial and formal design is based on the property's slope and an orientation in line with the cardinal directions. The slope of the roof faces the best side to get the most out of the photovoltaic panels. The timber house is designed as a simple cube, with a roof that slopes towards one corner – the entrance. Inside, the entrance platform is about 50 cm higher than the living-space level. The sleeping area and sanitary facilities are located on the open mezzanine floor. The building, whose façade is covered with larch wood, just like the interior space, features a southwest-facing terrace that offers a view of the beautiful surroundings.

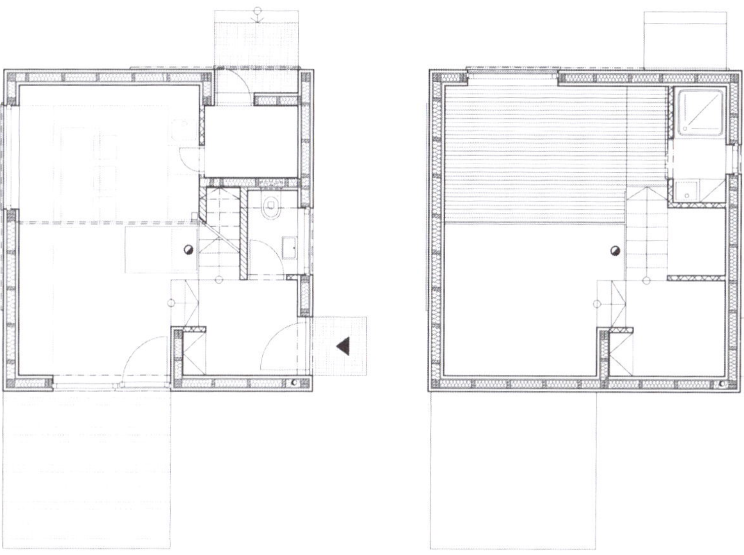

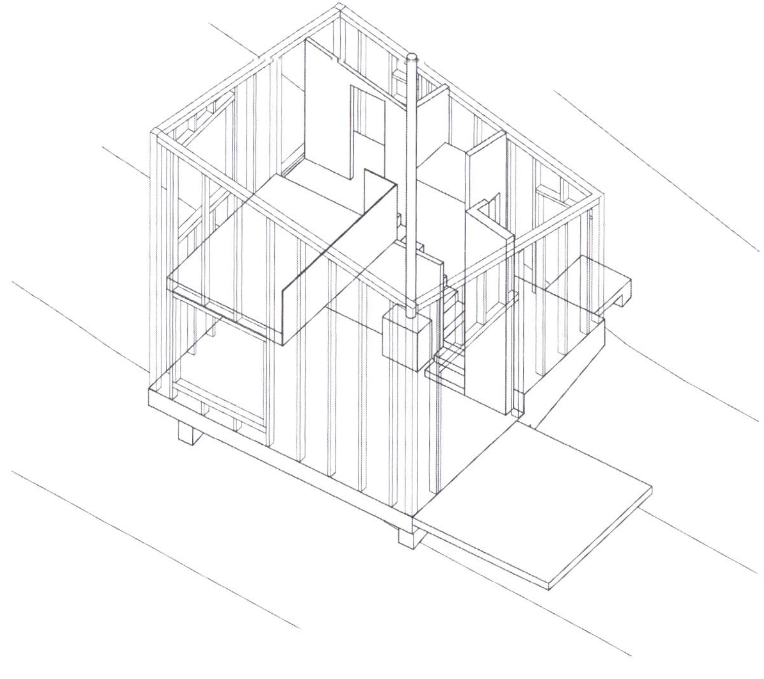

First Light Tiny Home

Wellington, New Zealand

Design
First Light Studio

Completion & Construction Time
2019 - 6 months

Client
Private

GFA
16.8 m^2 + 5.6 m^2 Mezzanine

Design Task
Transportable Tiny Home

Photographer
Build Tiny

For the First Light Tiny Home, the goal lay in creating a transportable sculptural object that feels as comfortable in motion as in a fixed location. The exterior is covered in smooth ebony, with matching aluminum joinery, lamps, and utilities. Due to the strict weight limits, the volume had to be distributed strategically to where it would be most valuable: The ridge of the asymmetrical gable sits above the bedroom in the mezzanine level. Six PV panels are placed along the lengthy roof surface, marking out the house's north-south axis. The ceiling-high French windows on one side and the sliding windows on the other ensure plenty of light and a view in all directions, regardless of the viewer's position.

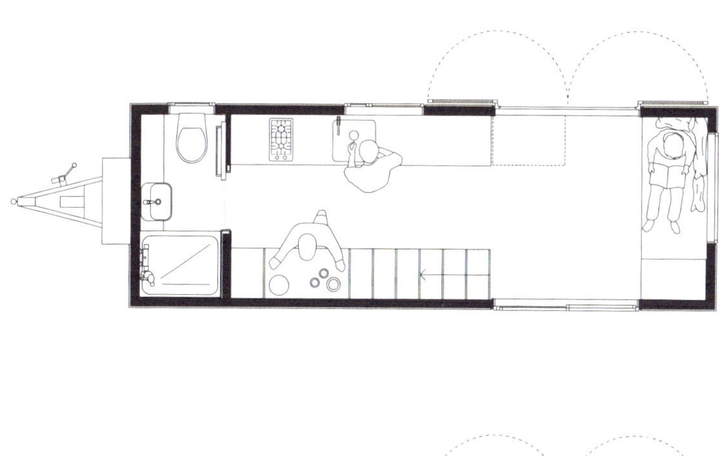

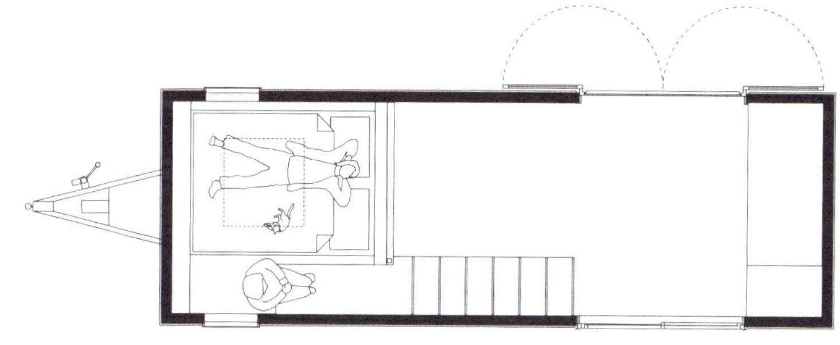

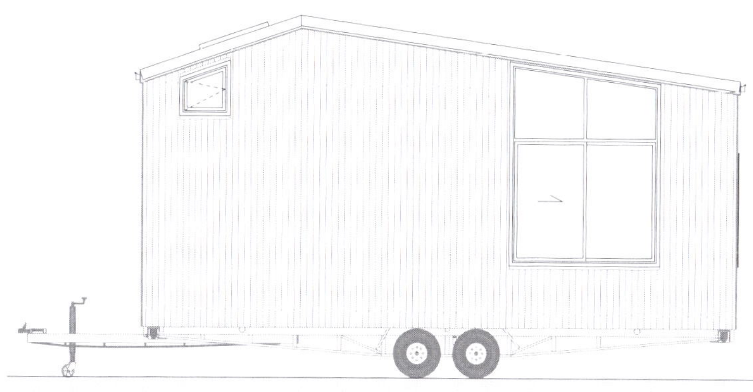

Piil

Jägala-Joa, Estonia

Design
Arsenit

Completion & Construction Time
2023 - 6 months

Client
Levstal Group

GFA
19 m^2

Design Task
Elegant prefabricated tree house

Photographer
Yifan Liu

The client asked for elevated "glamping" accommodation that could be used as a retreat or micro-hotel. Inspired by the observation towers dotted around attractive locations in Estonia, this tiny house hovers 4.25 meters above the ground, supported by a one-storey "leg" that incorporates a staircase, service facilities, and storage for sports equipment. The elevated bedroom offers more seclusion, a unique lookout point, and the possibility to rest between the branches. All of the house's elements are manufactured in a factory and then delivered to rural areas, where they are assembled into a complete structure.

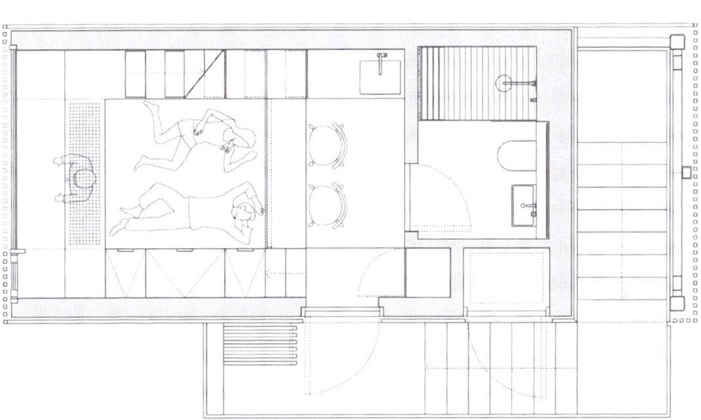

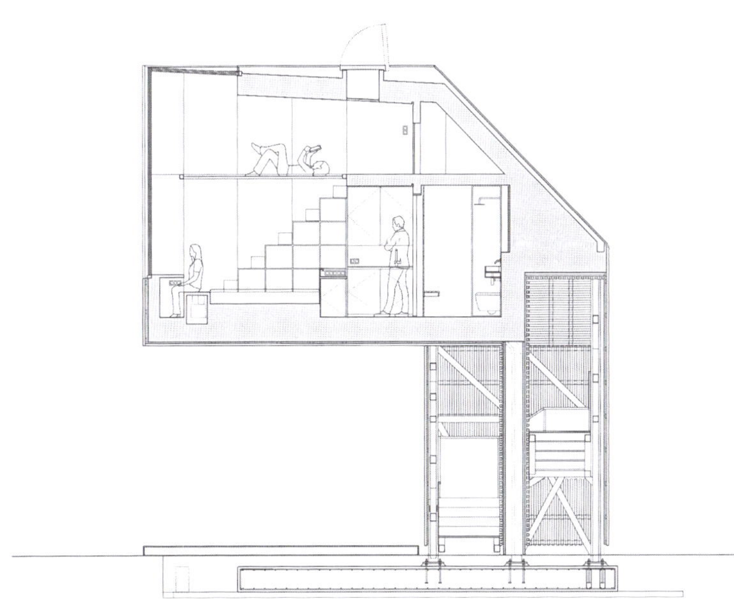

Cruachan Beag

Isle of Eriskay, Scotland

Design
BARD

Completion & Construction Time
2020 - 6 months

Client
Andy Laverty & Family

GFA
30 m^2

Design Task
Refurbishing and repurposing a stone ruin

Photographer
Liam Carlton, Alexander James-Aylin and BARD

Cruachan Beag demonstrates how ruins can be adapted to the landscape and redesigned to create contemporary architecture that does justice to both its past and its environment. A wooden frame was integrated into the existing stone walls. It is compact though has been carefully considered in its arrangement. Entry is by way of a small external courtyard formed to the rear. The effort of a series of turns allows the crescendo of the view to be unveiled to the visitor in a sequential manner. The east-facing skylights flood the interior with morning light. The exterior roof is covered with recycled Ballachulish slates and responds to the surroundings.

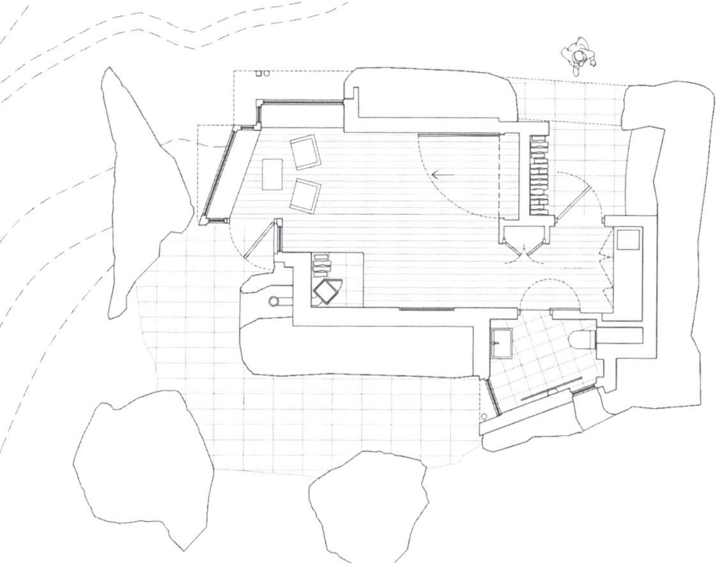

Little Black Cabin

Blue Mountains, Australia

Design
SMITH. Architects

Completion & Construction Time
2021 – 12 months

Client
Stewart Smith

GFA
28 m^2

Design Task
Salvaging a delapidated late 1800's timber cottage

Photographer
Clinton Weaver

Nestled in the breathtaking Blue Mountains in Australia, a century-old, dilapidated house has received a new lease of life – following its sustainable and carefully thought-out renovation, this spot now presents a modern house whose history has been preserved. Originally spanning 54 square meters, the size of the house has been reduced to 28 square meters by removing sections that were beyond saving. The design focused on efficiency and versatility. The remaining space was turned into a compact yet functional area, including a kitchen and living area, a sleeping area, a bathroom, and a laundry room. The windows have been designed to protect the building from bush fires. They ensure maximum privacy, offer the best view of the Blue Mountains, and provide optimal sunlight and cross ventilation. The building work is a response to the harsh natural environment.

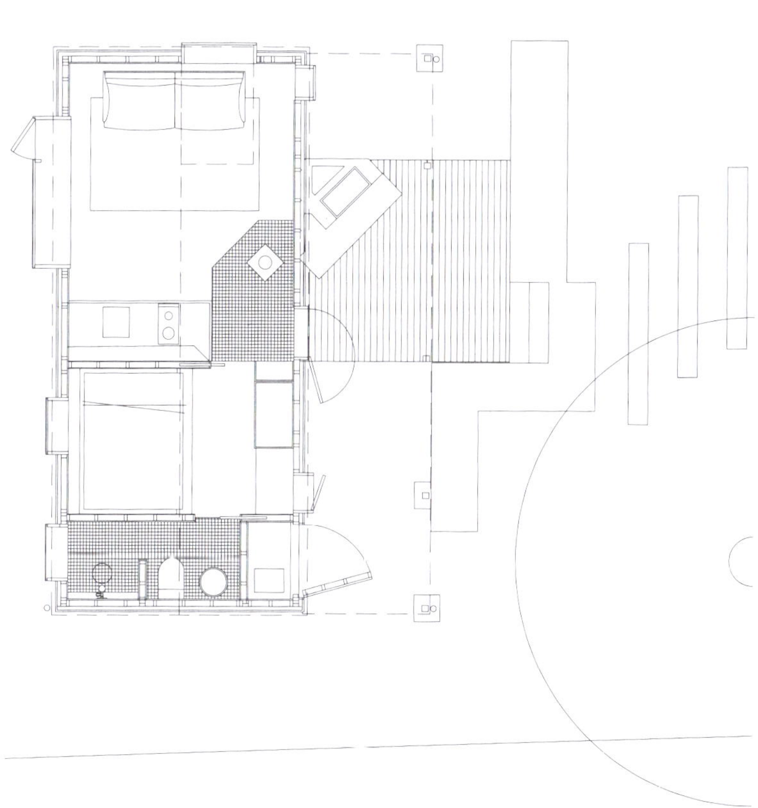

Litibu Bungalow

Nayarit, Mexico

Design
Palma

Completion & Construction Time
2020 - 6 months

Client
Private

GFA
50 m^2

Design Task
Design a litlle cabin in a beach town

Photographer
Palma

The 50 square meter bungalow on the Mexican Pacific Coast is characterized by a simple yet well-thought-out design with two subdivided areas, a public and a private one. A central courtyard connects the two. One key feature is the use of concrete. Extending beyond its structural role, concrete appears in built-in elements such as kitchen counters, shelves, and lintels, thereby blurring the boundaries between architecture and furniture. The exterior consists of rough concrete and greenish stucco that blends into the natural surroundings while at the same time drawing attention to the house.

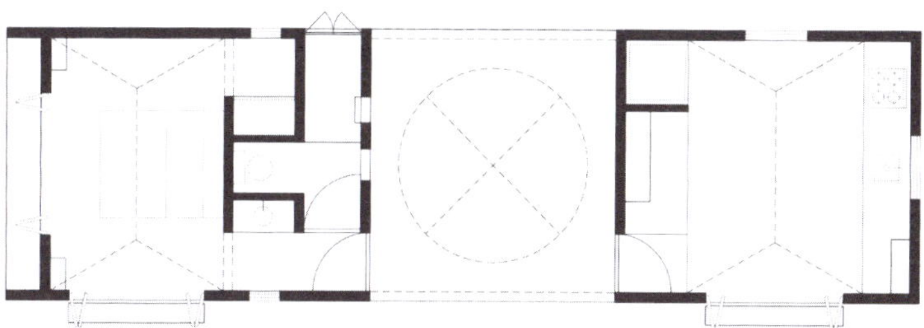

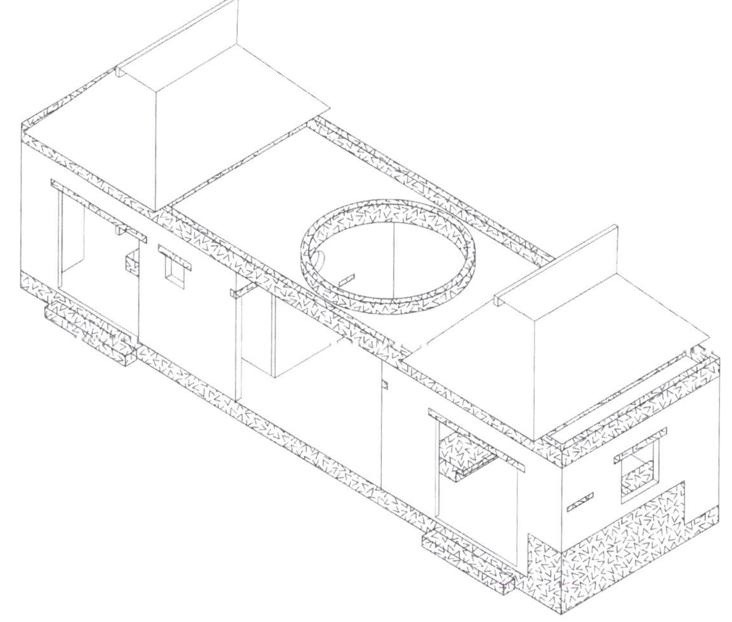

Cabin Moss

K□szeg, Hungary

Design
Béres Architects
Attila Béres, Jusztina Balázs

Completion & Construction Time
2021 - 24 months

Client
Attila Hideg

GFA
40 m^2

Design Task
Forest hideaway

Photographer
Tamás Bujnovszky

Cabin Moss is a tiny yet comfortable hut situated amidst hundred-year-old trees in the Alpokalja region, at the foot of the Alps. Spanning about 40 square meters, this little retreat offers plenty of living comfort. Supported by thin stilts, the building floats above the ground, while the windows create a playful motif, giving it a unique and memorable appearance. The building's exterior forms a stark contrast to its interior. The warm and cozy interior is draped in a coarse surface, allowing the forest to design the colors and patterns to its taste. One of the cornerstones of this project was the goal of keeping things small: no unnecessary surfaces, no remains, no wasted square meters.

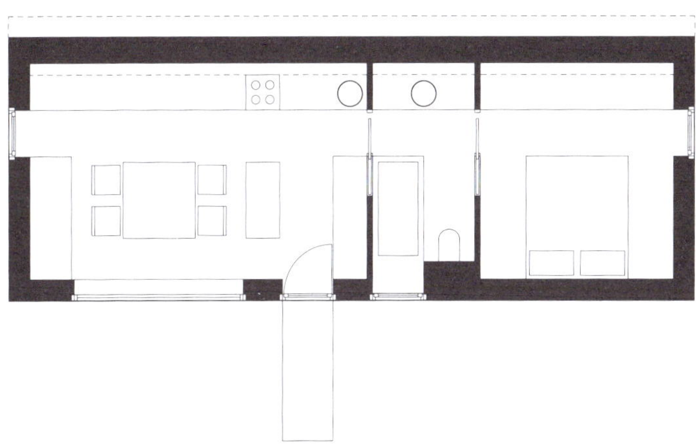

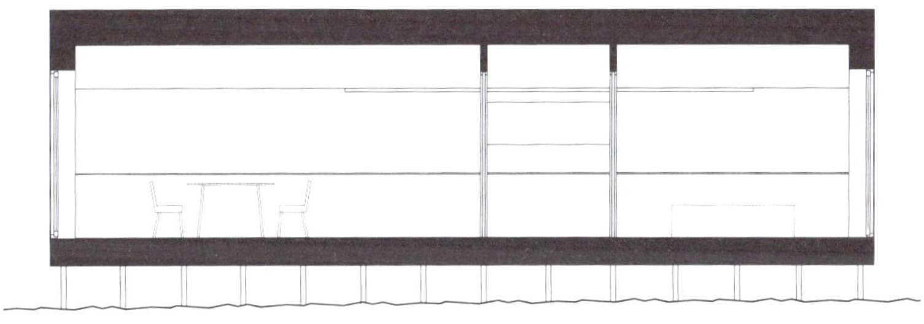

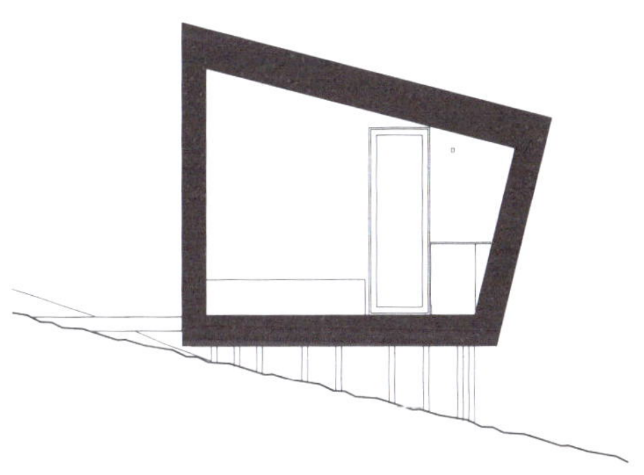

Tinyleaf

Okanogan County, USA

Design
GO'C

Completion & Construction Time
2023 - 24 months

Client
Private

GFA
30.66 m^2

Design Task
To design a compact cabin that blends seamlessly with the landscape and topography

Photographer
Ben Lindbloom

Tinyleaf lies embedded in a hillside in Washington's Methow Valley, just outside of Mazama. Building a strong relationship with the topography and responding to the very different seasons played a key role in the design. The cabin's south-facing façade features large, glazed sliding doors that let the landscape in. The flat roof offers more space on the roof terrace and keeps the snow at bay in the winter. The concrete exterior walls, which adopt the hues of the rocks, blend into the site's natural topography. The interior space is designed like a ship's cabin, with clever, hidden storage solutions. A small kitchen, bathroom, and bedroom present an efficient design, using shared storage solutions to separate the space.

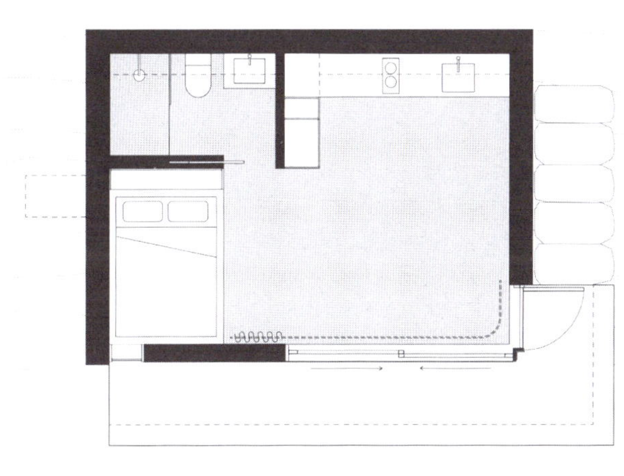

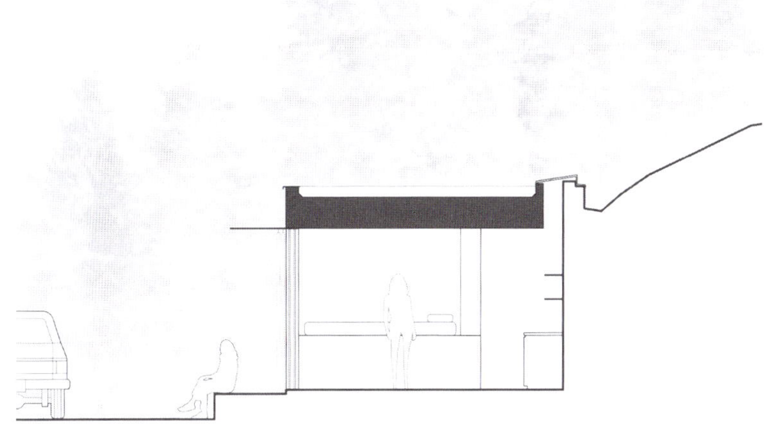

Index

The Deutsche Nationalbibliothek lists this publication in the Deutsche Nationalbibliografie; detailed bibliographic data are available in the Internet at http://dnb.dnb.de

ISBN 978-3-03768-306-4

www.braun-publishing.ch

1st edition 2025

Editor: Sibylle Kramer
Editorial staff and layout: Alessia Calabrò
Translation: Anja Wiest
Graphic concept: Sarah-Lea Hipp
Reproduction: Bild1Druck GmbH, Berlin

Product Safety
Publisher: Braun Publishing AG,
Arenenbergstr. 2, 8268 Salenstein, Switzerland,
publisher@braun-publishing.ch
EU-Representative: Bookwise GmbH,
Zeppelinstr. 67, 81669 Munich, Germany,
info@bookwise.de

Cover front: Jakub Hrab (photo left)
Rustam Shagimardanov (photo middle)
Mateo Pérez (photo right)
Cover back: Mateo Pérez (photo left)
João Carranca (photo right)